The Kitchen Gadget Cookbook

The Kitchen Gadget Cookbook

by

Annette Yates, Dianne Page and Jenny Webb

Contents

CHAPTER   PAGE

INTRODUCTION   7

MICROWAVE COOKING   9
1   Advantages and Limitations   11
2   The Microwave   14
3   Choosing a Microwave Oven   18
4   Containers for the Microwave   25
5   Using the Microwave   31
6   Adapting Your Own Recipes for Microwave Cooking   40
7   Using Recipes – Vital to All Readers   47
8   Microwave Cooking Techniques   50
9   Recipes   67

STEAMING   77
10   Introducing Steaming   79
11   At-a-Glance Guide to Steamers   81
12   How to Get the Best Results   87
13   Steam Cooking Techniques   90
14   Recipes   98

BLENDING AND PROCESSING   109
15   Blending   111
16   Getting the Best From Your Blender   117

17 Recipes for Blenders   121
18 Food Processors   130
19 Using Your Food Processor   136
20 Cooking Techniques with Food Processors   138
21 Care of Your Food Processor   150
22 Recipes   151

SLOW COOKING   161
23 Slow Cookers   163
24 How to Choose a Slow Cooker   166
25 Using a Slow Cooker   171
26 Getting the Best From Your Slow Cooker   176
27 Slow Cooking Techniques   183
28 Recipes   192

PRESSURE COOKING   203
29 Pressure Cookers   205
30 Using a Pressure Cooker   211
31 Cooking with Pressure   217
32 Recipes   238

FAN OVENS   251
33 Cooking with a Fan Oven   253
34 Using Conventional Recipes in a Fan Oven   254
35 Oven Temperature Conversion Chart   256
36 Using the Oven   258
37 Recipes   261

FREEZING   273
38 The Freezer   275
39 Checkpoints for Freezing   277
40 The Microwave/Freezer Friendship   279

INDEX   281

Introduction

Kitchen gadgets are wonderful things – particularly the big, expensive ones. So why do we buy them and then let them sit on the work surface, or worse still, at the back of the cupboard, not being used?

Quite often, because we can't quite work out how to fit them in to our routine. As a novelty the microwave, the slow cooker, the pressure cooker, the blender . . . is great, but soon we go back to the everyday grind which didn't include it before, and doesn't really include it now either.

That's where this book comes in. It will help you make the most of the gadgets in your kitchen and make them work for you to the best of their ability and the greatest of convenience to you.

It won't be long before you're using the equipment covered here to enhance your culinary life on a daily basis. Soon you'll be wondering how you *ever* got along without them!

Microwave
Cooking

1

Advantages and Limitations

Before buying a microwave oven, you need to know how it will benefit you and what it is capable of achieving.

What are the advantages of microwave cooking?

❖ Cooking times are much shorter. Conventional cooking times can be cut by as much as 60-75 per cent.

❖ Food can be thawed quickly using a microwave.

❖ It's economical. A microwave uses about 25 per cent of the power needed to run a conventional oven (a combination oven uses a little more). Added to this, cooking times are shorter and, when you make full use of a microwave, the lower the power level used, the lower the electricity consumption.

❖ It's versatile. Most foods can be thawed, cooked and reheated in a microwave.

❖ It's convenient. Snacks and meals can be prepared as and when they are needed. A microwave copes particularly well with small quantities and single portions, and in households where individuals eat at different times a microwave is a boon.

❖ It's easy to use. A microwave can be plugged in anywhere there is a 13 amp socket. Controls are generally straightforward to use.

❖ It saves on washing up, because many foods can be cooked in their serving dishes.

❖ It takes up a proportionally small space, making it very suitable for use in small kitchens and areas of restricted space for food preparation, such as bedsits. Microwave cooker sizes vary tremendously today, so you should always be able to find a model to suit your individual needs (see Chapter 3).

❖ Microwaves are clean and cool, and are particularly suitable for use by elderly and disabled people and children.

❖ Since there is no direct heat, foods are not baked or burned on to the containers (again, less washing-up!) or the inside of the oven: spillages can be cleaned easily with a damp cloth. (Combination cookers (see page 22) do tend to get more soiled than microwave-only cookers, because the oven walls heat up, although splashes – and therefore soiling – can be reduced by the use of roasting bags (see page 27).)

❖ Low-fat and fat-free cooking is easy with a microwave oven.

❖ Flavour and nutritive value are excellent in foods cooked in a microwave. Many foods can be cooked simply in their own juices; others with just a little additional liquid. Cooking foods for the briefest time, and in the least liquid, is known to be one of the best ways to retain maximum food value.

❖ Finally, you will find fewer cooking smells, less steam, and your kitchen cooking area remains cool.

Is there anything a microwave can't do?

❖ Browning and crisping are not possible unless the microwave oven has a grill or it is a combination oven (see page 22).

❖ Frying, either in shallow or deep fat, is not possible.

❖ It cannot successfully cook eggs in their shells.

❖ A microwave cannot make toast, unless it incorporates an efficient grill.

❖ It cannot make pancakes.

❖ A microwave cannot cook crusty pastry and bread, foods in batter, Yorkshire pudding, roast potatoes or soufflés, unless it is a combination oven (see page 22).

❖ Heating more than 300ml (½ pint) water is more economical in an electric kettle.

❖ A microwave cannot speed up the cooking of some foods. Rice, pasta and pulses, for example, generally take as long to cook in the microwave as they do conventionally.

To sum up
A microwave oven is invaluable when used not as an isolated appliance but as part of the team of cooking equipment in the kitchen. Used together with the hob, grill, kettle, toaster and conventional oven, a microwave oven will help you to get the best results in the shortest time.

2

The Microwave

What are microwaves and how do they cook food?
Cooking with microwaves is quite different from conventional methods which use electricity, gas or solid fuel. In a conventional oven the walls and the air inside them are heated first. As the oven heats up, so does the surface of the food. This surface heat, in turn, is slowly conducted to the centre of the food.

In a microwave oven the walls and air are not heated. The microwaves pass straight into the food, to heat it directly.

Microwaves are electromagnetic waves, similar to radio and television waves. Electric energy is converted into microwaves by a valve called a magnetron. The microwaves are channelled along a wave guide, then a stirrer or paddle distributes them evenly into the oven cavity. Once they are inside the oven, three things happen to the microwaves.

1. They are *reflected* off the metal walls and bounce around inside the oven cavity.

2. They are *transmitted* by glass, china, pottery, microwave plastics and paper. So the microwaves pass straight through dishes made of these materials.

3. They are *absorbed* by water (in particular) in food. When the water molecules absorb microwave energy they become agitated and vibrate at an incredible speed

– about 2,450 million times per second! It is this excitement which generates the heat which, in turn, cooks the food in a very short time. Microwaves can only penetrate food up to about 4cm (1½ in), so anything thicker than 8cm (3 in) relies on heat from the outer areas being conducted to the centre – just like conventional cooking.

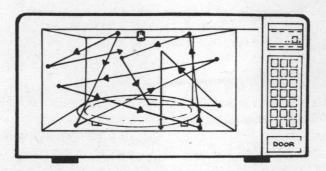

Fig. 1. The metal walls of the oven reflect the microwaves.

(Food is not shown in the oven for the purposes of this diagram, but remember, a microwave oven should never be switched on empty.)

Fig. 2. Certain cooking containers transmit microwaves.

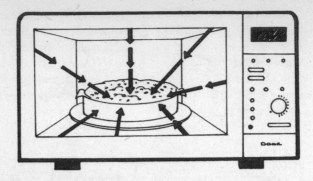

Fig. 3. Food absorbs microwaves and heats up.

Are microwaves safe?

❖ Microwaves produce a change in temperature only. They should not be confused with X-rays.

❖ Microwaves cannot be produced unless the oven door is securely closed. The doors and hinges are fitted with locks, seals and cut-out switches which automatically switch off the microwaves the instant the door is opened.

❖ The mesh in the oven door allows the cook to see inside the oven, but the holes in this mesh are not large enough to allow the microwaves to escape. They simply bounce off the mesh back into the oven cavity.

❖ British safety standards regarding the leakage of microwave ovens are extremely strict. Ovens are built to precise specifications and they are thoroughly tested before leaving the factory. When buying a microwave oven, look for the BEAB (British Electrotechnical Approvals Board) label for household appliances, which means that a microwave oven has met the safety requirements dictated by the relevant British Standard Specification for electrical safety and microwave leakage limits.

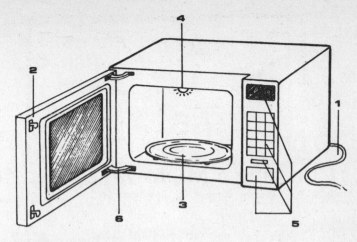

Fig. 4. The main parts of a microwave oven.

1. Lead from oven to 13 amp plug.

2. Door fastening. There may be two or more locking devices to ensure that microwaves are switched off as soon as the door is opened.

3. Removable shelf or turntable. This raises the food off the oven floor, so that microwaves can be absorbed from underneath too. It makes the job of mopping up spilled food easier and it also ensures that the food is in the best position to receive the microwaves (with a turntable, the food is carried around the oven to ensure even absorption of microwaves).

4. Interior light. This usually lights as soon as the oven is switched on.

5. Controls. Basic controls include an on/off button, a timer control and a control to adjust the microwave power level.

6. Door stop.

3

Choosing a Microwave Oven

Choosing a microwave oven is an exciting experience, so long as you are not intimidated by the vast choice on offer today. This section lists some of the questions worth answering before buying. It then goes on to outline many of the features available. Whether you are buying your first microwave or you are updating your current model, this should help you choose one which will fit in with the way you cook and eat.

How much do you want to spend?
Though price may dictate your choice initially, deciding which features you would like on an oven will also help to narrow down a price band.

How much space do you have and where?
Will the microwave sit on the kitchen work surface or on a shelf or brackets, or will you want it built into the kitchen? Most ovens need ventilation, so check you will be able to leave a space all round yours. Position the oven so that you have a small area of work surface next to it – for taking dishes out of the microwave and setting them down.

Will you want to move it around?
Maybe you will want to move it from one room to another, or perhaps outside. Maybe you will want to take it with you on

self-catering holidays. These points will dictate the exterior size of the oven and its weight too. Some table-top models can be very heavy. You will notice that all cookers are heavier on one side – usually the side containing the microwave-making valve (the magnetron).

How do you intend to use your microwave?
Will your microwave be restricted to thawing and reheating? If so, a basic model will be sufficient – a low wattage oven with cooking, heating and defrosting settings.

If, however, you will want to make full use of the microwave oven and cook all the things it does well – soups, snacks, sauces, fish, vegetables, poultry, casseroles, fruit and puddings – you will need at least 600W and several power levels (see page 49). Microwave cooking on a 500W machine will still be faster than conventional cooking, but if speed really is of the essence (and we all seem to get busier by the day!) then you may become frustrated with a lower wattage.

Are you likely to be preparing food in advance? Some models incorporate advance programming, enabling the microwaves to switch on while you are out. Some will keep your food warm on a heat-and-hold program.

Finally, if you prepare and cook a lot of cakes, pastry, roast dishes or oven-cooked food coated in breadcrumbs or batter you may like to consider buying a combination oven (see page 22) which combines the heat of a traditional oven with microwave cooking.

How many do you cook for?
Check the inside of the microwave oven. Is it large enough to take your largest casserole dish, or the largest item you are likely to cook? Will your dishes fit, and turn around, on the turntable? Even if you cook for one or two people most of the time, are you likely to cook for large numbers in the future?

Do you already have an efficient grill?
If not, you may consider buying a microwave oven which incorporates a grill (see page 22).

Do you have time to learn new processes?

More complex models are often said to take the thinking out of microwave cooking – with automatic sensors doing everything bar washing the dishes! Yet pre-set programs (some models have 20 or so) using the automatic sensor may not cook food to your liking. It can take far longer to learn and gain confidence in microwave cooking in a model which has an endless choice of programs. Despite this, these machines can prove indispensable to those who take the time to use and get to know them.

Do you have problems operating machines?

Elderly or disabled readers will find that microwaving is a convenient and safe way to cook. Touch-control models are easy to use and, for the visually disabled, some manufacturers can supply Braille panels. There is also a 'talking' microwave available.

Features on microwave and combination ovens

Controls can be mechanical or touch-control. Both are easy to use, but for accurate timing in seconds (for softening butter, for instance) choose a digital display. Touch-control panels are easy to wipe clean.

Oven interiors can be stainless steel or plastic-coated. Both are easy to clean, and personal preference will dictate which you choose. Combination ovens (see page 22) often have at least one self-clean lining; some top-of-the-range models have a pyrolytic cleaning function – the oven can be heated to a temperature which is high enough to burn off any food residue.

A *turntable* helps food to cook evenly by raising it off the oven floor so the microwaves can reach underneath, and by turning the food as it cooks. When buying a microwave with a turntable, check that your cooking containers and plates are not so large that they prevent the turntable turning.

Wave stirrers or paddles also encourage even cooking by distributing the microwaves evenly into the oven cavity. Some ovens have both a turntable and wave stirrers.

Power output indicates the amount of microwave energy used to cook food. It ranges from 500W to 1000W. The higher the wattage (W), the faster the microwave cooks. Recipes in magazines and books (including this one), and cooking times on many pre-packed foods, are generally based on 600-700W. If you buy a more powerful oven, you will need either to reduce the cooking time by about 25%, or to lower the power level to the equivalent of 600-700W and cook for the normal time. If you buy a 500W model you will need to lengthen cooking times by about 30%.

Power levels control the amount of microwave energy entering the oven, so food can be cooked as quickly or as slowly as you like. Manufacturers vary in the way they describe power levels – some have up to nine settings but the most useful are HIGH (100%), MEDIUM-HIGH (75%), MEDIUM (50%), MEDIUM-LOW (30%) and LOW (10%).

A *shelf* allows more food to be cooked at the same time, though cooking times will be longer. The same amount of microwave energy goes into the oven, no matter how much food it holds, and this energy has to be shared out.

An *auto-minute* button is handy. Just press it to cook for 1 minute on HIGH (100%).

Quick/Rapid/Jet start or *Boost* is designed for quick heating of liquids, and drinks in particular. It usually works on a higher power than that used for everyday cooking.

A *minute timer* or alarm can sometimes be used as an automatic timer, with no cooking involved.

Auto-defrost is a useful feature, though most foods can be thawed on DEFROST or MEDIUM-LOW (30%). Auto-defrost is controlled either by time or by the weight of the food. Some models have a sensor which weighs the food and automatically calculates the thawing time.

Auto cook/heat allows you to program in the type of food and its weight, then the oven does the rest – calculating the cooking time, appropriate power levels and, in combination ovens, the temperature. Some models have an automatic sensing device which does this. This auto-cook/heat feature is particularly useful for large pieces of meat and for ready meals.

Hold-warm puts the oven on a low power level to keep food warm for 15 minutes or more.

Multi-sequence cooking allows you to program the oven to cook on a series of cooking times and power levels – for example, cooking on HIGH (100%) for a set time, switching to MEDIUM (50%) for a set time, then holding on LOW (10%) for a set time.

Auto-repeat recalls the last program used.

A *memory* function stores programs – useful only if you cook the same dishes frequently.

Delay-start/Pre-set/Auto-start delays cooking for several hours if necessary, perhaps while you are out. This feature is more useful in a combination oven (for conventional or combination cooking) than in a microwave where cooking times are very short anyway and food may need turning or stirring.

A *grill* is useful for improving the appearance of micro-waved food, and if you do not already have an efficient conventional grill. Don't expect a grill in a microwave oven to be as powerful as a conventional grill, though, and it is likely to operate only with the door closed. Some ovens allow simultaneous grilling and microwaving to save time. Grills with radiant elements are similar to conventional electric grills. Halogen bulbs give instant heat, though they are usu-ally restricted to only one area of the oven ceiling. A quartz grill is both quick and efficient.

A *combination oven* combines the speed of microwaving with the traditional heat of a conventional oven. Foods can be browned and crisped as well as cooked in a fraction of the usual time. A combination oven is particularly useful if you regularly cook whole poultry and meat joints, pastry, cakes, Yorkshire pudding, soufflés, and other foods which need a crisp and brown finish.

As the name suggests, a combination oven can be used in three ways: on microwave only, on convection only (using traditional heat in °C), or with a combination of the two (often called 'combination', 'dual-cook' or 'Hi-speed'). It is when cooking on 'combination' that models vary in the way they work. There are three main types:

❖ Where both the temperature and the microwave power level can be controlled by you.

❖ Where the temperature can be controlled, while the microwave power level is pre-set.

❖ Where there are a series of pre-set programs in which specific temperatures are already matched up with selected microwave power levels.

Your choice will depend on whether you are a keen cook who likes to experiment, and who prefers to be able to adjust temperature and microwave power in order to achieve the results you want; or whether you prefer to have it all selected for you, ready simply to press a button.

Rotisserie units feature in some combination ovens, for cooking meat and poultry on a spit, using a combination of microwaving, grilling and convected heat.

An extra word on choice

When making your final choice, it is worth asking to see the instruction books and cook books which accompany the ovens. Some are better than others.

Microwave labels

A voluntary labelling scheme for microwave ovens and food packs was introduced in 1992. It was developed by the then Ministry of Agriculture, Fisheries and Food (MAFF) in partnership with oven manufacturers, food manufacturers, retailers and consumer organisations. It is designed to help us to microwave food more successfully, particularly when heating small quantities of food, such as ready meals for one or two.

New microwave ovens are now labelled with:

❖ The power output of the oven, based on an internationally agreed standard (IEC 705).

❖ A heating category letter, from A to E, to indicate the oven's ability to heat small food packs.

Fig. 5. The microwave labelling scheme.

1. Microwave symbol.
2. Power output (watts).
3. Heating category for small packs.

The aim is for all small (up to 500g) food packs which are suitable for microwaving to be marked with the microwave symbol plus appropriate heating category letters and cooking times. Then, you simply match up the information on the food pack with that on your microwave oven.

4

Containers for the Microwave

The containers which are suitable for microwave cooking are those which allow microwaves to pass straight through them into the food. You'll probably find that many of the dishes you already own will be fit for use in the microwave. Those which have their own lids are the most convenient.

What to use
Ovenglass, glass ceramic, china and glazed pottery and stoneware are suitable. Although they let microwaves pass through them, you will probably still need to use oven gloves to lift them from the microwave oven, because the heat conducted from the food makes the dishes hot. For this reason, dishes used for cooking must be able to withstand the heat created by the food contained within. Also, because they absorb a lot of heat from the food, cooking in these containers may take slightly longer than in materials which are specially designed for the microwave.

A wide range of microwave cookware is available today, not only in heat-resistant plastic, but also in ovenglass and ceramic glass. The most versatile are suitable for microwave, conventional oven, freezer and dishwasher. They are usually fit for cooking foods which reach a very high temperature, such as those containing a high proportion of fat or sugar. Always check the labels before buying and, if your model has a turntable, make sure the cookware fits on it, and that it will turn freely. Look out for useful starter sets of microwave cookware – an economical way of buying the most useful items.

Paper, soft plastics and basketware should only be used for brief heating. Kitchen paper can be used to absorb moisture during microwaving but don't use the recycled variety as it may contain minute traces of metal.

What not to use
Metal containers reflect microwaves and, in general, should not be used when microwaving.

Some microwave manufacturers suggest using small pieces of foil to shield food and prevent it overcooking – follow the instructions carefully. Others suggest cooking some foods in foil trays – do check with the instruction book and follow the method carefully. If the manufacturer of your oven does not advise it, don't do it – if anything were to go wrong, your guarantee would be affected.

Do not use plates or dishes which are decorated with gold, silver or metal paint. The microwaves will cause the metal to spark and blacken.

Avoid using unglazed or partly-glazed pottery, fine glass (it contains minute particles of metal), polystyrene, dairy product containers, dishes which have been repaired with glue (the glue may melt) and mixing bowls with rubber on the base (again, it may melt!).

To test if a container is suitable for the microwave
Put the dish in the microwave oven and place a cup containing 150ml (¼ pint) cold water inside it. Cook on HIGH (100%) for 1-2 minutes. The outer dish should remain cool while the water in the cup heats up. If the dish becomes warm, it has absorbed some of the microwaves and is unsuitable for use.

The shape matters
Circular containers are best because the microwaves reach the food equally from all sides. Though the centre usually cooks more slowly than the edges, stirring food during cooking encourages even results.

A *ring* shape produces best results and is particularly useful for foods which cannot be stirred – like cakes. There is no slow-cooking centre, so the food cooks evenly.

Squares and rectangles tend to overcook at their corners, where the microwaves are concentrated. They often have an area in the centre which cooks only slowly.

A *bowl* is a useful container – it has no corners so the microwaves enter the food fairly evenly. It is particularly suitable for foods which cannot be stirred (sponge puddings, for instance) and for sauces.

Straight sides on a container help the food to cook evenly. Sloping sides allow microwaves to concentrate in, and over-cook, food at the outer edge.

Food wraps

Roasting bags and *microwave bags* are useful for microwave cooking. Follow the packet instructions for use. (Ordinary polythene food bags are not suitable.) They are particularly suitable for microwaving small quantities of soup, casseroles and for reheating plated meals. They can be used in the microwave, in the conventional oven (up to a specified temperature), as a boil-in-the-bag, and for freezer storage. When microwaving, sit the bag of food in a small, rigid container (to keep it an even, uniform shape) and tuck the open ends under loosely so that steam can escape.

Boil-in-the-bags are also resistant to high temperatures and are useful for single portions in the microwave, for boiling on the hob and for freezing. Some commercially frozen foods and pre-prepared products are supplied in these bags which make them ideal for microwave cooking. Always remember to make a small slit in the bag to prevent it ballooning up (and possibly bursting) and to allow the steam to escape.

Cling film can be used to cover dishes when no suitable lid is available, but do not allow it to touch the food. Pierce it, or turn back a small area, to allow steam to escape during cooking.

Absorbent kitchen paper, greaseproof paper and *non-stick paper* are useful for wrapping or covering foods.

	Microwave Cooking	Freezing	Microwave Defrosting	Microwave Reheating
Oven glass, e.g. Pyrex	Yes	Yes	Yes	Yes
Glass ceramic, e.g. Pyrosil	Yes	Yes	Yes	Yes
China/porcelain (not those with decorative metal borders)	No	No	Yes	Yes
Stoneware	Yes	Yes	Yes	Yes
Pottery (glazed only – test for suitability first, see page 26)	Yes	No	No	Yes
Glass (not crystal)	No	No	No	Short term only
Ovenable board (semi-disposable dishes)	No	No	No	Short term only
Basketware	No	No	No	Short term only
Cling film	Covering only	Heavy duty freezer film	Covering only	Covering only
Boil-in-bags (pierce before microwaving)	Yes	Yes	Yes	Yes

	Microwave Cooking	Freezing	Microwave Defrosting	Microwave Reheating
Freezer bags (120-200 gauge)	No	Yes	Yes	No
Roasting bags	Yes	No	No	Yes
Plastic (only use types specifically for use with boiling water – if they are dishwasher safe they should be suitable for use in the microwave)	Some	Yes	Yes	Short term only – unless specifically designed for microwave use
Plastic foam cups and plates	No	No	Yes	Bread products only
Paper cups and plates	No	No	Yes	Yes
Paper towels, serviettes	Covering and absorbing moisture only	No	Covering and absorbing moisture only	Covering and absorbing moisture only

Do not use the following materials in the microwave oven: Metal and foil containers (some containers are lined with foil, so take care); conventional oven thermometers.

Useful accessories

A *microwave rack* or *trivet* is handy to encourage even cooking of all foods – to raise dishes in the oven so that the microwaves can easily reach the food from every direction. They are also useful for thawing meat and other foods, preventing them from sitting in a pool of liquid. In microwave cookers with metal turntables, it is particularly important to raise the food and these cookers usually have a special rack supplied with them. Simply sit the food or dish on the rack. They are also useful for cooking joints of meat – the meat is raised above its juices, to promote 'roasting' rather than 'stewing'.

Browning dishes are useful in microwave-only ovens. They have a special coating which heats up in the microwave, for searing and browning small items such as bacon, sausages, steaks, chops, eggs, fish, vegetables and toasted sandwiches. The surface of a browning dish can reach a temperature of up to 300°C (600°F). Always use oven gloves, follow the dish manufacturer's instructions carefully and never exceed the recommended pre-heating time. Once the food is put on the hot surface, cooking is completed by microwaving. A browning dish is particularly useful for imitating shallow frying of meat, sausages, bacon, eggs and 'toasted' sandwiches.

A *plate ring* is useful for stacking plated meals for thawing or reheating in the microwave. Best results are obtained if no more than two plates are stacked.

A *jug* for heating liquids and for making sauces. Even when cooking small quantities there must be room for the liquid to rise or boil up in the jug, so choose a larger one than you would normally think necessary. A good size jug also allows plenty of room for stirring or whisking sauces before, during and after cooking.

A *microwave thermometer* is particularly helpful for successful thawing and cooking of meat and poultry and is specially designed for use while the microwaves are switched on. Other thermometers should *only* be used while the microwave cooker is switched off. Some microwave cookers have a special thermometer or probe attached to the cooker cavity. It is inserted into the food during cooking and the microwaves switch off automatically when it has reached the required temperature.

5

Using the Microwave

A microwave oven is a versatile piece of equipment which thaws, cooks and reheats food at a moment's notice. As you get to know your oven, you will discover that several things affect thawing/cooking/reheating times and the way the microwave performs generally:

❖ The type of food, its moisture content (the more it contains, the longer it takes to cook) and its density (dense foods, like meat, take longer to thaw than porous foods such as bread and cake).

❖ The quantity of food – two potatoes take longer to cook than one, though not necessarily double the time – for this reason, avoid filling the microwave with food.

❖ Its shape and size – regular shapes cook more evenly than irregular shapes, and small pieces cook quicker than large pieces.

❖ The starting temperature of the food dictates how long it takes to thaw/cook/reheat – for instance, food from the refrigerator takes longer to cook than food at room temperature.

❖ The container used – and its shape in particular – a circular shape with straight sides is best (see page 26).

❖ The power level used – the higher the power level, the faster the cooking.

❖ The way in which food is cooked conventionally – food which normally requires slow, gentle cooking will benefit from cooking on a low power level in the microwave.

❖ The arrangement of the food – even layers encourage even heating; arrange individual foods in a circle with thicker areas towards the edge of the dish; turning, stirring and repositioning foods encourages even results too.

❖ The standing time – most foods should be allowed to stand for a short time after microwaving – to allow the temperature to even out and to allow the food to finish thawing, cooking or reheating.

DEFROSTING FOOD

The ability to thaw foods in minutes is one of the great advantages of the microwave. The need for advance meal planning is not so urgent, and it matters little if you forget to take food out of the freezer or if unexpected guests turn up on your doorstep. A meal can still be ready for eating in next to no time.

The DEFROST or MEDIUM-LOW setting is used to thaw frozen foods. This usually applies microwave energy to the food in short bursts – a clever technique since a continuous burst of microwaves would result in areas of melted food heating up with adjacent parts remaining frozen. The DEFROST/MEDIUM-LOW control ensures even thawing, allowing heat from the melting parts to be conducted to the colder areas during the rest periods when the microwave energy is off. (See page 49 for a guide to power settings and their uses.)

Generally, thawed foods require a *defrosting-standing time* when the temperature inside the food is allowed to even out and any remaining ice crystals can melt normally. By allowing for this *defrosting-standing time* you will make sure that thawing is even and that the food does not begin to heat up or cook at its edges. Many microwave cookers have an AUTO-DEFROST setting which is controlled by time, during which the microwaves start thawing on a high power, gradually reducing to the lowest power, to thaw the food efficiently. It is designed so that the thawing times effectively include a *defrosting-standing time*.

Some models have AUTO-DEFROST which is weight-controlled – taking the guesswork out of thawing. You program in the type of food and the cooker automatically calculates the thawing time (and often the *defrost-standing time*). In the latest models you simply put the food in the microwave and a crystal beneath the turntable automatically calculates the weight of the food and its thawing time.

Not all foods need thawing, however. Some can be cooked from frozen. Vegetables are the best example. To ensure even thawing and cooking, stir or shake them once or twice during microwaving.

Tips for defrosting

❖ Microwave-to-freezer containers save washing-up. Cook, freeze, defrost and reheat in the same container.

❖ Frozen vegetables need no defrosting – they can be cooked straight from the freezer.

❖ Freeze food in shallow blocks – they will defrost more quickly.

❖ Remove metal ties, foil or foil containers before defrosting.

❖ Open containers and bags before defrosting to prevent them splitting or bursting open. The air inside will expand as it warms up.

❖ Remove giblets from inside poultry as soon as possible.

❖ Place cakes, bread and pastries on kitchen paper during defrosting, so excess moisture is soaked up.

❖ Before defrosting, remove any excess ice which may be attached to the food.

❖ Defrost frozen foods in a close-fitting dish. If the thawed areas are allowed to spread over the base of a container they will attract more of the microwave energy and consequently over-heat. When freezing food it is a good idea to line the container with a roasting bag, or microwave bag, before putting in the food. This way the frozen block can be lifted out and packed away in the freezer – useful if you don't have a never-ending supply of microwave-freezer dishes.

❖ Cover foods (except baked foods such as cakes, bread and pastries) to hold in the heat and speed up the defrosting time.

❖ Follow manufacturer's instructions for defrosting times until you are familiar with your microwave. It is a good idea to note down times for quantities of food which you will regularly wish to defrost.

❖ Separate large pieces of food such as sausages and chops as they thaw, to encourage quick, even defrosting.

❖ Turn or rotate food during defrosting. This is done automatically if your oven has a turntable or stirrers. Large items such as joints of meat and whole poultry will require turning over at least once during defrosting to encourage even thawing. Legs and thin areas may be covered with foil pieces to prevent cooking. Check with your manufacturer's instruction books regarding the use of foil. It is essential to allow some *defrosting-standing time* before cooking to allow the temperatures to equalise (see comments on AUTO-DEFROST setting, above).

❖ Make sure poultry and meat are *completely* thawed before cooking.

❖ Finish defrosting poultry by immersing it in cold water during the *defrosting-standing time*. Defrosting completely in the microwave oven usually causes outer areas to begin to cook while the centre (the giblet bag) is still frozen. It is essential to defrost poultry and meat *completely* before cooking.

❖ Use a microwave thermometer to tell you when the centre of a joint has thawed. Unless it is a special microwave oven food thermometer, do not leave it in the oven during defrosting or cooking.

❖ Pour off liquid from meat and poultry which is being defrosted in its bag. The liquid slows down defrosting by absorbing the microwaves.

❖ Break up foods such as liquids, soups, sauces and casseroles during defrosting. Use a fork or spoon and stir occasionally once defrosting has really started. Packages which do not allow for breaking up or stirring should be flexed to spread the heat – for example boil-in-the-bag foods. (Remember to pierce the bag to let out expanding air and steam.)

❖ If commercially frozen foods are packed in foil, decant into suitable close-fitting containers before defrosting. (Some frozen prepared foods come in packaging which is suitable for microwaving, but check cooking instructions on the packet to be sure.)

❖ Some foods do not need rest periods during defrosting – small pieces of food such as left-overs, pastries, cakes, fish fillets and single bacon rashers can be subjected to a short continuous period of defrosting on HIGH.

❖ Food frozen at home usually takes longer to defrost than commercially frozen food. The ice crystals tend to be larger and require more energy to thaw.

❖ When plating meals for the freezer, make sure that the food lies within the edge of the plate. Do not overlap food. Thicker, denser items should be arranged towards the outer edge.

❖ Defrosting times will vary according to the food's shape, weight and density and its storage temperature in the freezer. Your instruction book will give you details for your particular model. Remember it is always preferable to *underestimate* defrosting times. If the food is not completely thawed after the *defrosting-standing time* then it may simply be returned to the microwave oven for a short time longer (allow a short time for standing too).

❖ If food begins to feel warm – even if only in one patch – stop thawing and allow it to stand for several minutes before starting again.

REHEATING FOOD
Food reheats efficiently in a microwave, in a fraction of the time taken conventionally; and its colour, texture and flavour can be just as good as freshly-cooked food.

Tips for reheating
❖ The colder the food, the longer it will take to heat – food from the refrigerator takes longer than food at room temperature.

❖ Avoid reheating large, solid items, such as a joint of meat. Results are more successful if it is sliced first.

❖ Arrange food with care – in shallow, even layers. A plate of food should be arranged so that there is one even layer, with thick, dense items towards the edge.

❖ Two plated meals can be reheated by stacking one on top of the other, with a plate ring between them. Turn the plates (in opposite directions) at least once during reheating.

❖ Cover or wrap food during reheating – to retain heat and moisture so that it heats evenly and quickly. Bread, pastry, crumble toppings and similar foods which need to be kept dry, should be reheated uncovered.

❖ Some foods benefit from reheating on MEDIUM (50%) or MEDIUM-LOW (30%) – such as vegetables and slices of sponge or Christmas pudding. Large pieces of food which cannot be stirred (like lasagne) should be reheated on MEDIUM (50%). Foods with plenty of moisture and foods which can be stirred are usually suitable for reheating on HIGH (100%).

❖ Stir foods whenever possible during reheating – such as soups, sauces, casseroles, milk puddings and drinks.

36

Turn or reposition large items at least once – such as poultry or meat pieces, whole potatoes, lasagne, moussaka and shepherd's pie.

❖ Always under-estimate reheating times to avoid over-heating food. It is preferable to put the food back in the oven to heat for a little longer, rather than spoil it.

❖ Make sure that reheated food is *piping hot throughout*.

❖ Use a food thermometer if you want to make sure that the centre of the food is hot.

❖ Always allow food to stand after reheating – to allow its temperature to even out.

❖ Some foods improve with reheating – casseroles and soups in particular but also slightly stale bread which freshens on reheating.

❖ Pastry and crunchy toppings can lose their crispness if overheated, so heat them carefully.

❖ Take care when heating pastry with a filling. Although the pastry may feel only warm to touch, the filling is usually much hotter.

CARE OF YOUR MICROWAVE

Look after your oven and follow the manufacturer's instructions and it will reward you with years of reliable service. Avoid operating the oven while it is empty – make sure by keeping a small container of water in the oven in case someone switches it on in error. Do not use metal containers in the oven (unless the manufacturer allows this), do not allow anything to jam in the door (tea towels, for instance) and never lean heavily on the door. Lastly, make sure that every member of the household knows how to operate the oven correctly.

Keeping a microwave oven clean is usually a simple matter of wiping out the oven after each use. The walls of the oven don't heat up during cooking, so food does not bake on them as it does in a conventional oven. This is not the case with a combination oven, however, which does heat up and, because the cavity is smaller than a conventional oven and the oven walls are closer to the cooking food, splashes can easily burn on.

Tips for cleaning microwave and combination ovens

❖   Wipe out the interior frequently and regularly.

❖   Mop up spills and splashes as soon as they occur – spilled food and splashes will only slow down the cooking the next time the oven is used.

❖   Removable parts, such as a turntable or a shelf, should be washed with hot water and detergent, then thoroughly dried.

❖   For heavy soiling, put a bowl of water in the microwave oven and cook on HIGH (100%) until it boils – the steam produced will help to soften stubborn marks, which can then be wiped away with a soft cloth.

❖   To remove lingering odours from the oven, add some lemon juice to the water.

❖   Do not use abrasive cleaners on any part of a microwave or combination oven, and never use a knife to clean off a stubborn mark.

❖   Never allow water or cleaning materials to enter any vents in the oven cavity.

❖   To clean stubborn stains from a combination oven, use liquid cleaners only.

❖   Look for specially-designed microwave oven cleaners too.

Replacement parts

In the event that an oven part needs replacing (such as a turntable, shelf or bulb), obtain it from an authorised service agent. To find out your nearest one, contact the manufacturer of your oven (the address and telephone number should be in your instruction book).

If a fault occurs
Always obtain qualified help – from an authorised service engineer. Never remove the outer casing of the oven or attempt to repair a fault yourself.

Servicing
If you use your oven correctly and do not move it around frequently or drop it, there's little need to have it checked. However, if you have reason to believe that the oven has been damaged in any way, or if you notice a change in its performance, you may wish to have it checked by an authorised engineer. Many manufacturers offer a service contract on new ovens.

Leakage testing
If you look after your oven, there is little need to have it checked (see above). A microwave oven which has been damaged sufficiently to allow leakage (by dropping it, for instance) will not work. However, once people start to wonder whether their oven leaks, for whatever reason, mistrust lingers and minds should be put at ease by having the oven checked over by a qualified engineer.

Over recent years consumers have been tempted to buy low-cost hand-held leakage testers. They have all proved to be unreliable. At the time of publication, there is still nothing as dependable as those used by authorised engineers and environmental health officers. Their testers are substantial and costly machines which are recalibrated regularly to make sure they are accurate.

6

Adapting Your Own Recipes for Microwave Cooking

Many of your own everyday recipes will be suitable for cooking in the microwave. Here are some general guidelines.

Timing
The obvious difference between microwave cooking and conventional cooking is the timing. As a general rule, cook your favourite recipes for one quarter to one third of their usual cooking time. For example, a dish which takes 40 minutes to cook conventionally may take about 12 minutes to cook in the microwave. There will, of course, be foods which do not fit into this rule so it is a good idea to under-estimate times and check the dish often when trying it for the first time. Remember that under-cooked food can be put back in the microwave to finish cooking, but over-cooked food cannot be corrected. Compare the cooking time of your recipe with a similar one in your manufacturer's instruction book. After all, no one knows your particular model better than its manufacturer. Always be guided by this until you are confident of success. Use the ingredient with the longest cooking time as your guide to overall timing too.

It is worth remembering that the following points will affect the timing.

❖ *The type of food.* Foods containing moisture generally cook better than dry ones. The more moisture the food contains, the longer it will take. Adding water to moist foods also lengthens the cooking time. Dense foods take longer than porous foods – for instance, a solid piece of meat takes longer than the same quantity of minced meat. Extra cooking time on a low power will be needed for tenderising tougher cuts of meat or for foods which need to absorb a lot of moisture (for example, rice and dried foods). Foods which usually require gentle, slow cooking when prepared conventionally should be cooked on MEDIUM (50%).

❖ *The quantity of food.* Two whole potatoes will take longer than one (though not twice the time) because the microwave energy has to be shared between the two items. If your microwave has a shelf, two layers of food can be cooked, but, again, the cooking time will be longer. On the whole, food on the lower level tends to cook more slowly, so foods with shorter cooking times should be positioned there. Generally, though, avoid filling the microwave with food – with whole potatoes, for example. It is usually quicker to heat or cook them in small amounts.

❖ *Its shape and thickness.* Perhaps the most important point to remember when preparing ingredients is to cut all meat and vegetables into even sizes, as regular shapes cook more evenly. It is a good idea therefore to bone and roll irregular-shaped joints of meat. Thinner pieces of food cook faster than thick ones so, when appropriate, cut large pieces into smaller pieces to allow the microwaves to penetrate them faster.

❖ *The arrangement of the food.* If meat slices or pieces of fish are piled up in a cooking container they will cook unevenly. Make sure they are evenly distributed in the container. Arrange wedge-shaped foods with the tail end towards the centre (e.g. asparagus, small fish fillets). Tuck the thin ends of fish fillets under each other and overlap fish tails to produce a more even layer of food.

When putting cooked meals on a plate for reheating later, make sure the arrangement is even (with no high piles of potatoes, for example, and with delicate foods, such as meat slices, placed in the centre of the plate).

❖ *Its starting temperature.* Food at room temperature will cook in less time than food from the refrigerator or freezer. Cooking times given in this book are for foods at room temperature. Check that the food is cooked after the minimum time – it can always be microwaved for a little longer if necessary. Do, however, make sure that the food is piping hot throughout.

❖ *The container used* and its shape in particular. A regular shape with vertical sides is best (see Chapter 4).

❖ *The power level used.* Power levels enable you to adjust the amount of microwaves entering the food. Use the chart on page 49 as a guide.

Some microwave cookers incorporate sensors. These devices enable the cooker to switch off when the food is cooked – by sensing its temperature, either on its surface, or in the surrounding atmosphere. Other cookers may include computerised programs for specified weights of individual foods or made-up dishes. Check to see if the food or dish you are preparing is included in these. If not, use the manual settings, following the advice given above.

Cooking-standing time
Always allow for a cooking-standing time. Food continues to cook after the microwaves are switched off as the heat is conducted from the hot outer areas of the food to the cooler central areas. Large dense foods require longer cooking-standing times. Joints of meat, for instance, will keep hot and go on conducting heat to the centre for 15 to 30 minutes after the microwave energy is switched off. Other foods may need only a few minutes' cooking-standing time, e.g. scrambled egg could be removed from the microwave when it is still slightly

wet and under-cooked – by the time it is served, it will have finished cooking and firmed up.

With a little patience and practice, cooking times will become second nature and you will begin to gauge small differences automatically.

Turning and stirring food

Food cooked in a microwave needs to be turned and/or stirred to ensure even cooking. Avoid positioning small pieces of food in a circle with one in the centre – the one in the centre will tend not to cook. Soups, vegetables, sauces and casseroles need to be stirred occasionally to encourage even cooking. Turn foods like whole fish, chicken pieces and whole potatoes once during cooking and re-position foods such as meatballs from the outside of the dish to the centre.

Drinks should always be stirred before putting them in the microwave and part way through heating, to prevent them suddenly bubbling over.

Browning food

Generally speaking, food cooked by microwaves does not brown. Unlike conventional cooking, the heat which cooks the food is not directed on to its surface, so it does not dry out, harden and brown. This 'drawback' seems to become less important as you get to know your microwave, improve your methods, use attractive garnishes and even change your attitude to crisp and browned food. You will probably find that you prefer some foods without browned surfaces. Fish, vegetables, soups, sauces, casseroles and puddings are all good examples of foods which do not need browning but which cook superbly in the microwave.

Many microwave cookers have a browning element, or grill, which can be used to brown the tops of dishes. A combination cooker cooks with microwaves and convected heat simultaneously – producing crisp, brown food in a fraction of the conventional cooking time.

Browning dishes

These are designed specifically for microwaves. They are the only containers which can be heated empty in the microwave.

Their special coating absorbs the microwaves (on HIGH/ 100%), reaching a temperature of up to 300°C/600°F. The food (particularly meat, sausages, eggs, fish, vegetables and toasted sandwiches) is placed on the hot surface to sear and brown. Cooking is then completed by microwaving in the same dish. Always use oven gloves when using a browning dish, and protect your work surfaces with a heat-resistant layer before placing the hot dish on them.

Follow manufacturer's instructions carefully when using browning dishes and never exceed the recommended pre-heating time.

Microwave and roasting bags

These are excellent for cooking larger joints of meat and whole poultry in the microwave. Tie the bag loosely to allow steam to escape during cooking. To promote browning, allow plenty of air between the meat and the bag and allow space for the bag to expand during cooking. It is a good idea to slit the bag in several places under the joint and then place the meat on a rack in a tray – as the meat cooks, the juices drain away. Alternatively, split the bag open and use it to cover the joint (which is placed on a rack, tucking the ends under).

Using roasting bags in combination cookers can help to keep the cooker walls clean and free from splashes. Follow the advice in your microwave instruction book (see page 27).

Browning agents

These can be sprinkled or spread on to food to produce an appearance similar to conventionally cooked food. But beware: some of these flavour the food too, so they should be chosen with care to complement the food.

Sauces such as soy, barbecue, brown, fruity, and Worcester-shire can be used, as can soup and gravy mixes or stock cubes or granules. However, each of these will alter the natural flavours and should be used carefully. Paprika mixed with melted butter gives excellent results when brushed over whole chicken. Glazes using honey, jams, chutneys, mustard, soy sauce or tomato purée look (and taste) good on pieces of chicken, beef, lamb or pork.

Toppings and colourings

Dishes such as casseroles and sauce-covered vegetables can be made more attractive in various ways. They can be browned under the grill before serving (make sure the container is suitable). Alternatively, sprinkle them with toasted or fried breadcrumbs, grated cheese (particularly Parmesan), chopped fresh herbs, chopped nuts or grilled or fried bacon pieces.

Sweet dishes can be topped with brown sugar, chopped nuts, ground spices and so on. The colour of cakes can be improved by using wholewheat flour, treacle, brown sugar, spices, chocolate, cocoa or coffee in the ingredients. Simple decorations such as a sprinkling of icing sugar or cocoa powder will disguise a pale surface, as will the addition of icing with chopped nuts, grated chocolate, glacé cherries, etc.

Healthy eating with your microwave

Whether you are on a strict diet – such as low-calorie, low-fat, salt-free – or whether you are generally aiming for a healthy diet, the microwave can be an asset.

Foods cooked in the microwave often retain more of their flavour than foods cooked conventionally. Not only do they cook quickly so there is less chance of destroying vitamins, but also the majority of foods can be cooked using a little (and sometimes no) liquid, with less chance of washing away certain vitamins.

Since foods mainly cook in their own juices there is hardly ever need to add fat in microwave cooking. The true fresh flavours are retained and foods do not stick to the cooking containers.

Individual portions are quick and easy in the microwave, involving less effort (and fewer cooking utensils) than conventional cooking. So if someone in your family is trying to cut down on calories, fat, or sugar, for example, it need not entail the preparation of a special menu for one. In fact, as time goes by, you will probably discover that you have slowly moved over to a more healthy diet as you increase the number of dishes prepared in your microwave.

Checklist for converting recipes for microwave cooking

❖   Reduce the cooking time to about one third.

❖   Cook for the minimum time, rather than over-cook – check the cooking progress often until you are confident and ensure that the food is piping hot throughout.

❖   Check with a similar recipe in your instruction book.

❖   Cut ingredients into even sizes.

❖   Reduce the liquid in soups and casseroles by about a quarter. If necessary add extra during or after cooking.

❖   Use little or no fat. It is not needed to brown or to prevent sticking.

❖   Use less salt and spicy seasonings. Adjust seasoning after cooking if necessary.

❖   Choose your power level.

❖   Arrange food evenly.

❖   Stir or cover foods which would normally need stirring or covering during conventional cooking.

❖   Add delicate or quick-cooking ingredients towards the end of cooking.

❖   Use quick-cooking or ready-cooked alternatives when possible, e.g. canned kidney beans and quick-cooking rice.

❖   When doubling recipe quantities, increase the cooking time by a quarter to one third.

❖   When halving recipe quantities, decrease the cooking time by about one third.

7

Using Recipes –
Vital to All Readers

Cooking times

Cooking times are affected by the output (or wattage) of the microwave oven. Recipes created in a 600-700W microwave oven (as are those in this book) will take longer to cook in any machine of less than 600W while any machine over 700W will cook them quicker. If your model differs in output from that used to generate the recipe, adjust the timings accordingly. Here is a brief guide:

Up to 600W	*600-700W*	*750W and over*
40 seconds	30 seconds	20 seconds
1½ minutes	1 minute	50 seconds
4 minutes	3 minutes	2½ minutes
6½ minutes	5 minutes	4 minutes
13½ minutes	10 minutes	8½ minutes
20 minutes	15 minutes	12½ minutes
27 minutes	20 minutes	16½ minutes

Variable powers

Alternatively, if your microwave has a higher wattage simply use a lower power level which is the equivalent of that used to create the recipe (check with your instruction book) and cook for the recommended time.

See the table opposite for a general guide to power settings and their uses.

Measures
Where recipes are included here, measurements are given in metric and imperial. Use one type for best results.

Spoon measurements are level unless otherwise stated.

Eggs used are size 3 unless otherwise stated.

To cover or not to cover
When you want to retain moisture (e.g. in casseroles, steamed sponge pudding), cover with a lid, a plate or pierced cling film. When keeping in the moisture would spoil the dish (e.g. fruit crumble, bread), leave uncovered. If you can't decide, it probably doesn't matter anyway!

Covering food may prevent some sensors from operating properly. If your microwave cooker has a sensor, check with your instruction book to see if cling film should be used (or indeed if food should be covered at all).

Power level:	LOW	MEDIUM-LOW	MEDIUM	MEDIUM-HIGH	HIGH
Equivalent watts (approx.):	10%	30%	50%	70-75%	100%
	60-70W	200-250W	300-350W	400-525W	600-700W
Use for:	Keeping food warm. Softening butter. Melting chocolate. Rising yeast doughs. Very gentle thawing.	Thawing. Gentle simmering. Developing the flavour of sauces and casseroles. Gentle cooking of casseroles, soups, custards, rice and solid foods such as lasagne.	Boost thawing. Simmering sauces, casseroles and soups. Cooking and reheating solid foods, such as cottage pie. Some puddings and cakes. Cooking critical ingredients, such as eggs, cream or cheese.	Reheating foods. General cooking of small quantities of foods. Some puddings and cakes.	General cooking of fish, vegetables, fruits, tender cuts of meat, poultry and sauces without cream or eggs.

8

Microwave Cooking Techniques

SOUPS AND STARTERS

Home-made soups are quick and easy in a microwave, whether you are making an individual portion or enough for a family.

Anyone who likes to make the occasional pot of good home-made stock will find it convenient to put the broken-up bones, chicken carcass or well-washed vegetable peelings into a bowl, cover them with water and cook for about 30 minutes (or more, if preferred). When the mixture is strained, you have a delicious fresh stock ready for adding to sauces and, in particular, to soups.

Tips for cooking soups

❖   Use a large, deep bowl so that the soup has plenty of room to boil up. This is particularly important when a recipe contains milk.

❖   When cooking a conventional soup recipe in the microwave, reduce the quantity of liquid by about one quarter. There is usually less evaporation in the microwave. If the finished soup is too thick, it can always be diluted after cooking.

❖   Cut ingredients such as vegetables into even pieces to encourage even cooking. The smaller they are cut, the quicker they will cook.

❖ The cooking time can be speeded up by adding *boiling* water or stock to the main ingredients (a kettle boils a large quantity of water far more efficiently than a microwave). To speed up cooking even further, use half the liquid only, then add the extra (hot) after cooking.

❖ Cover soup to keep the moisture and heat in. A lid with a vent helps to prevent it boiling over. If you don't have a vented lid, put a wooden cocktail stick between the bowl and lid.

❖ Stir the soup occasionally to encourage even cooking.

❖ Most soups can be cooked on HIGH (100%). Remember, the cooking time will depend on the ingredient with the longest cooking time.

❖ If a soup contains meat which requires tenderising, rice, pasta or other cereals, it will cook just as quickly if it is first brought to the boil on HIGH (100%), then cooked on MEDIUM (50%) or MEDIUM-LOW (30%) for the remaining time. In the same way, a soup can be left to simmer gently for as long as you wish, to develop its flavour, just as you would leave it on the hob.

❖ *Dried soups:* Make up the soup mix with hot water (from the kettle) following the packet instructions. Cook on HIGH (100%) stirring occasionally, until the soup boils. Lower the microwave power to MEDIUM (50%) or MEDIUM-LOW (30%), cover and cook for the time stated on the packet, stirring occasionally.

❖ *Cans and cartons of soup:* Pour the soup into a bowl, diluting it according to the label instructions if necessary. Cover and cook on HIGH (100%), stirring occasionally, until hot.

FISH

Fish is made for the microwave! It cooks quickly, keeps its shape beautifully and retains all its juices. Cook it whole or in fillets; just as it is, brushed with butter, or in a sauce. No matter which method you choose, so long as you don't overcook it, the texture and taste are wonderful.

Tips for thawing fish

❖ Thaw fish on DEFROST or MEDIUM-LOW (30%).

❖ Cover it to ensure even thawing.

❖ Separate pieces and reposition them as they begin to thaw.

❖ Take care not to overheat or the fish will start to cook around the edges. If any areas start to feel warm, stop thawing and allow the fish to stand for 5-10 minutes before continuing.

GUIDE TO THAWING TIMES	
Type of Fish	**On DEFROST or MEDIUM-LOW (30%)**
Whole round fish	4-6 minutes per 450g (1 lb)
Whole flat fish	3-4 minutes per 450g (1 lb)
Cutlets, steaks and fillets	3-4 minutes per 450g (1 lb)
Prawns and shrimps	2-3 minutes per 100g (4 oz)
	3-4 minutes per 225g (8 oz)
Scallops	3-4 minutes per 225g (8 oz)

Tips for cooking fish

❖ Make a few slits in the skin of whole fish. This allows steam to escape and prevents the skin from bursting open.

❖ Use a shallow dish, unless you are cooking fish in a sauce, casserole or soup.

❖ Arrange fish in an even layer to encourage it to cook evenly. When cooking whole fish, overlap their tails, or lay them side by side with head to tail. With fillets, either roll them up and secure them with a wooden cocktail stick, or tuck the thin ends underneath the thick ends to achieve an even layer. When cooking fish steaks, arrange them with the thinner ends towards the centre of the dish.

❖ Season with salt after cooking to prevent the fish drying out and the surface from toughening.

❖ When cooking with butter, best results are achieved if it is melted first and brushed over the fish.

❖ Cover during cooking, to keep the moisture in.

❖ Turn whole fish once during cooking.

❖ Take care not to overcook fish. Shellfish cooks especially quickly and is easily overcooked – for this reason add it to a dish towards the end of cooking.

❖ Should you find that fish easily overcooks on HIGH (100%), try using a lower power level and cooking for slightly longer.

❖ Check that fish is cooked by lifting up the flakes with a fork. If it is still slightly undercooked, just lay the flakes back down again and allow the fish to stand and the temperature to even out – the flakes should turn opaque and cook to perfection.

❖ Allow cooked fish to stand for 3-5 minutes before serving.

❖ *Boil-in-the-bag* fish can be cooked in its bag. Remember to pierce the bag before cooking.

❖ *Fish in breadcrumbs or batter* is generally not suitable for microwave cooking, though fish fingers are acceptable when cooked on a browning dish (follow the dish manufacturer's instructions).

GUIDE TO COOKING TIMES

Type of Fish	Per 450g (1 lb) on HIGH (100%):
Whole round fish	4 minutes
Whole flat fish	3 minutes
Steaks, cutlets and thick fillets	4-6 minutes
Thin fillets	2-3 minutes
Prawns, raw	2-4 minutes
Scallops, shelled	2-3 minutes, adding corals for final 1-2 minutes

Tip: If you find that fish cooked on HIGH (100%) tends to spit and overcook, try reducing the power to MEDIUM (50%) and cooking for a little longer.

Fish – Basic method

1. Put the fish in an even layer in a shallow dish. If wished, brush with melted butter, or add 30ml (2 tablespoonfuls) water, stock, milk or wine.

2. Cover and cook, using the times above as a guide.

3. Allow to stand for 3-5 minutes before serving.

SAUCES

Sauces are quick and easy to make in the microwave because they can be cooked in a serving jug or bowl. Even small quantities cook well without sticking or burning, as they often do in a saucepan on the hob. Most sauces reheat well in the microwave too.

Tips for cooking sauces

❖ Use a jug or bowl which is large enough to allow the sauce to boil up.

❖ Don't bother to cover the container – you need to stir the sauce often and a cover can be a nuisance.

❖ Most sauces can be cooked on HIGH (100%), but those containing eggs are best cooked on MEDIUM (50%) or MEDIUM-LOW (30%) to prevent them curdling.

❖ Stir sauces frequently during cooking to prevent lumps forming.

❖ To develop the flavour of a cooked sauce (such as tomato sauce), or to thicken or reduce it further, continue cooking, uncovered, on MEDIUM (50%) or MEDIUM-LOW (30%) until the desired flavour and consistency are achieved.

❖ Reheat sauces on HIGH (100%), stirring occasionally.

❖ *Frozen sauces* can be reheated straight from the freezer. Put the frozen block in a bowl and cook on HIGH (100%), breaking up the sauce as it thaws. Once it has thawed, stir or whisk the sauce occasionally during reheating.

MEAT AND POULTRY

Meat and poultry can be thawed and cooked in the microwave oven. It is particularly suitable for bacon rashers and joints; whole poultry and poultry pieces; minced meat; and cubes of beef, pork, lamb, bacon and poultry for cooking in a sauce.

The results with joints of meat, chops and steaks depend on personal taste, unless you have a combination oven (which browns and crisps as well as cooking quickly with microwaves). Here, you will find plenty of tips on how to get the best results.

Tips for thawing meat and poultry

❖ Remove any metal tags from the wrappings.

❖ Stand the meat or poultry on a microwave or roasting rack – to lift it above the liquid which collects beneath.

❖ Thaw on DEFROST or MEDIUM-LOW (30%).

❖ Separate items like bacon rashers, chops and steaks as they begin to thaw. Reposition them occasionally too.

❖ Turn large pieces, joints and whole birds over at least once during thawing.

❖ Pour away any moisture as it collects around the meat or poultry during thawing. If you don't, the liquid will heat up while the rest remains frozen.

❖ If any areas begin to warm up, stop thawing and allow a standing period of about 20 minutes before continuing.

❖ When thawing is completed, allow small pieces to stand for at least 10 minutes before cooking. Large pieces, whole poultry and joints need at least 30 minutes.

GUIDE TO THAWING TIMES	
Type of Meat	Per 450g (1 lb) on DEFROST or MEDIUM-LOW (30%):
Beef joints, on bone	10-12 minutes
Boneless	8-10 minutes
Beef, steak	8-10 minutes
Lamb joints	5-6 minutes
Pork/bacon joints	7-8 minutes
Chops	8-10 minutes
Cubed & minced meat	7-10 minutes
Liver & kidney	7-9 minutes
Chicken, whole	6-8 minutes
Turkey, whole	10-12 minutes
Chicken & turkey portions	5-7 minutes

Tips for cooking meat and poultry

❖ Thaw meat and poultry completely before cooking.

❖ Regular shapes, such as boned and rolled joints, cook more evenly than irregular shapes, such as a leg joint.

❖ Meat on the bone cooks more quickly than off the bone.

❖ Secure large items with string or with wooden (not metal) skewers.

- ❖ Season with salt *after* cooking, to prevent the surface from drying and shrinking. If the meat or poultry is immersed in liquid, a little salt can be added prior to cooking.

- ❖ Put large pieces and joints on a microwave or roasting rack, so they do not sit in their juices during cooking.

- ❖ A browning dish is useful for cooking chops and sausages (follow the dish manufacturer's instructions).

- ❖ Arrange small pieces, like chops or chicken drumsticks, with their thinner ends towards the centre of the dish.

- ❖ Arrange small even-shaped pieces, such as meatballs, around the edge of the dish.

- ❖ Meat loaves cook best in a ring-shaped mould.

- ❖ Cover during cooking to keep moisture in, to help the meat or poultry to cook evenly, and to keep the oven walls free from splashes.

- ❖ Cover joints or whole poultry with a split roasting bag, to encourage a little browning of the surface.

- ❖ Joints and whole poultry are usually cooked on HIGH (100%) (see *Tip* below the cooking guide overleaf). Meat and poultry which is immersed in liquid can be brought to the boil on HIGH (100%), then cooked on MEDIUM (50%) or MEDIUM-LOW (30%) until the meat or poultry is tender – just like boiling and simmering on the hob.

- ❖ Turn large pieces, whole poultry and joints at least once during cooking.

- ❖ Stir casserole-style dishes occasionally during cooking.

- ❖ Check that meat and poultry is cooked by inserting a skewer into the thickest part. The juices should always run clear from pork and poultry, though you may prefer them pink in beef and lamb. If you use a meat thermometer, insert it into the thickest part of the meat and make sure it does not touch any bone.

❖ Allow joints and whole poultry to stand for 15-20 minutes after cooking – to allow the temperature to even out and to make carving easier.

GUIDE TO COOKING TIMES	
Type of Meat	**Per 450g (1 lb) on HIGH (100%)**
Beef, rare	5-6 minutes
medium	6-7 minutes
well done	8-9 minutes
Lamb, medium	7-8 minutes
well done	8-10 minutes
Pork	8-10 minutes
Bacon	9-12 minutes
Liver & kidney	6-8 minutes
Chicken, whole	8-10 minutes
Turkey, whole	9-11 minutes
Chicken & turkey portions	6-8 minutes

Tip: If you find that meat and poultry cooked on HIGH (100%) overcooks, try cooking on HIGH (100%) for the first few minutes, then reducing the power to MEDIUM-HIGH (75%) or MEDIUM (50%) until cooked through.

GUIDE TO COOKING TIMES	
Meat, portions	**On HIGH (100%)**
Chops, 1	2-4 minutes
2	3-5 minutes
3	4-6 minutes
4	5-7 minutes
Bacon rashers, 2	2-3 minutes
4	4-5 minutes
6	5-6 minutes
Chicken breast, boneless	2-3 minutes

EGGS AND CHEESE

Eggs and cheese are popular choices for a quick snack, breakfast, lunch or supper. Both do well in the microwave, so long as they are cooked gently and carefully.

Tips for cooking eggs

❖ Do not try to cook an egg in its shell – steam builds up beneath the shell, making it explode, even after the microwaves have been turned off.

❖ Eggs which are at room temperature give the best results.

❖ Prick the yolks of eggs which are to be left whole during cooking, to prevent them from bursting open.

❖ Avoid overcooking eggs – they become tough. Always stop cooking before the egg or eggs are fully cooked – they will finish cooking during a short standing time.

❖ If eggs cook too quickly on HIGH (100%), better results may be achieved by using MEDIUM (50%) power.

Tips for cooking cheese

❖ Add cheese to a dish towards the end of cooking when possible, to prevent it overcooking and becoming stringy.

❖ Cheese melts quickly and evenly if it is grated rather than sliced or diced.

❖ If cheese cooks too quickly on HIGH (100%), better results may be achieved by using MEDIUM (50%) power.

VEGETABLES

Fresh vegetables cooked in the microwave are simply delicious. Because they are cooked quickly and in the minimum amount of liquid, they retain their full flavour and colour, and cook to the stage where they are still slightly crunchy. Small quantities of vegetables are very successful too, cooked in a small dish so there is no saucepan to wash up.

Cooked vegetables also reheat well in the microwave – to look and taste as if they had only just been cooked.

Tips for cooking vegetables

❖ Use good quality vegetables for best results. Old, tired vegetables will toughen and dry out.

❖ Choose even-sized vegetables for cooking whole. Otherwise, cut them into even-sized pieces to encourage even cooking.

❖ Prick the skins of whole vegetables in several places before cooking, to prevent them bursting open.

❖ Frozen vegetables can be cooked straight from the freezer.

❖ Arrange whole vegetables in a circle, to encourage them to cook evenly. Avoid putting one in the centre.

❖ When cooking more than 450g (1 lb) cut vegetables, best results may be obtained if they are cooked in batches.

❖ Add 45-60ml (3-4 tbsp) water to the vegetables. Root vegetables and old vegetables often need more. Extra water may also be needed if you want to cook vegetables until they are very soft.

❖ Season vegetables with salt *after* cooking or they will become dry and tough.

❖ Cook most vegetables on HIGH (100%). If they tend to overcook or shrivel, it may be preferable to cook on a slightly lower power, such as MEDIUM-HIGH (75%).

❖ Cover cut vegetables during cooking to keep the moisture in.

❖ Stir, shake or turn vegetables occasionally to encourage them to cook evenly.

❖ Cooking times will depend on the type and quantity of vegetables as well as their age. As a guide, 450g (1 lb) cut vegetables take 7-10 minutes. Always underestimate the time and test in the usual way – by inserting the tip of a knife.

❖ Whole vegetables, such as potatoes, need to stand for several minutes before serving, to allow the temperature to even out.

RICE, PASTA, PULSES AND CEREALS

The cooking of rice, pasta and pulses is not necessarily quicker in a microwave. However, microwaving is certainly a convenient and clean method.

Instant breakfast cereals and porridge are quick and convenient too, particularly when individual portions are prepared in the microwave.

Tips for cooking rice, pasta and pulses

❖ Use a large deep bowl, to allow the contents to boil up.

❖ Adding a little oil to the cooking water helps to prevent it from boiling over.

❖ Large quantities, over 450g (1 lb), are best cooked conventionally on the hob.

❖ Always add boiling water to the rice, pasta or pulses. Boil the water in a kettle to save time.

❖ Salt can be added to the cooking water of pasta. Rice and pulses are best seasoned with salt *after* cooking, to prevent them from toughening.

❖ Though covering during cooking keeps moisture in, results are just as good if no cover is used – and there is less chance of the contents boiling over and flooding the floor of the microwave.

❖ Stir well after adding the boiling water, before cooking.

❖ Rice need not be stirred again, but pasta and pulses should be stirred occasionally during cooking.

❖ Allow a standing time of 5 minutes before serving.

Pasta – Basic method

1. Put the pasta in a large, deep bowl with salt and a little oil, if wished. Pour over sufficient boiling water to cover the pasta by at least 2.5cm (1 in). Stir well.

2. Cook for:
   3-4 minutes for 225g (8 oz) fresh pasta
   7-10 minutes for 225g (8 oz) dried pasta
   10-14 minutes for 450g (1 lb) dried pasta.
   Stir occasionally during cooking, to prevent the pasta pieces sticking together. Stop cooking when the pasta is still slightly undercooked.

3. Stir well, cover and allow to stand for 5 minutes before draining and serving.

Pulses – Basic method

1. Soak 225g (8 oz) pulses in plenty of cold water overnight. Alternatively, pour plenty of boiling water over the pulses, cover and allow to stand for 1-2 hours. (Split peas and lentils do not need soaking before cooking.)

2. Drain and put the pulses into a large bowl and pour over enough boiling water to cover them by at least 2.5cm (1 in).

3. Cook, stirring occasionally, until tender.
   Aduki beans: 30-35 minutes
   Black-eye beans: 25-35 minutes
   Cannellini beans: 30-45 minutes
   Chick peas: 50-60 minutes
   Flageolet beans: 35-45 minutes
   Haricot beans: 25-35 minutes
   Lentils: 20-30 minutes
   Mung beans: 20-30 minutes
   Peas: 30-45 minutes
   Red kidney beans: 30-45 minutes
   Split peas: 20-30 minutes

4. Cover and allow to stand for 5 minutes before draining and using.

FRUIT AND DESSERTS

Fruit is perfect for cooking in the microwave, staying in shape and retaining all its juice, flavour and colour. Light sponge and suet puddings are cooked in minutes instead of taking hours of steaming on the hob. Crumbles, cheesecakes, milk puddings and egg custard are all ideal candidates for microwave cooking too, and don't forget to use the microwave to dissolve gelatine and to melt chocolate for mousses and other desserts.

Tips for cooking fruit

❖   Pierce or split the skins of whole fruits, such as apples, to prevent them bursting open.

❖   Frozen fruit can be cooked straight from the freezer.

❖   Add water to hard fruits and fruits with skins, such as apples and plums. 45-60ml (3-4 tbsp) is a good guide.

❖   Soft fruits, such as raspberries and blackcurrants; fruits with a high water content, such as rhubarb; and apple slices for a purée, usually need no additional liquid.

❖   Either dissolve sugar in the cooking liquid or add sugar after cooking. Do not sprinkle sugar over fruits with skins, such as plums or blackcurrants, or the skins will toughen.

❖   Cover during cooking, to keep the moisture in and to help the fruit cook evenly.

❖   Most fruit can be cooked on HIGH (100%), but if it tends to overcook or burst open, try lowering the power to MEDIUM (50%). The difference in the cooking time will be minimal.

❖   Cooking times depend on the type, quantity and age of the fruit. As a guide:
450g (1 lb) soft fruit takes 2-5 minutes
450g (1 lb) hard fruit takes 7-10 minutes.

❖   Stir gently or reposition whole fruit occasionally during cooking.

❖ Allow to stand for 3-5 minutes before serving.

Tips for cooking sponge and suet puddings

❖ When cooking a conventional recipe in the microwave, add extra liquid to the mixture. A good guide is to add about 15ml (1 tbsp) per egg.

❖ Use a pudding bowl which is large enough to allow the pudding to rise up.

❖ A transparent bowl allows you to see when the pudding is cooked.

❖ Lightly grease the bowl before adding the pudding mixture.

❖ Cover the pudding loosely with a 'hat' of greaseproof or non-stick paper, to keep moisture in and to allow the pudding to rise above the top of the bowl if necessary.

❖ Stand the bowl on a microwave rack or an upturned saucer, to encourage even cooking.

❖ Cook on HIGH (100%) for 3-7 minutes, depending on the size of pudding.

❖ Stop cooking when the surface of the pudding is still slightly moist, but the mixture beneath it is cooked. The surface will dry as the pudding stands.

❖ Allow to stand for 3-5 minutes before turning the pudding out, to let it settle.

❖ Turn the pudding on to a warmed plate.

❖ If the bottom of the pudding is still slightly under-cooked, do not put it back into its bowl. Put the plated pudding back into the microwave and cook briefly until set.

Tips for cooking milk puddings

❖ Use a large, deep bowl, to allow the pudding to boil up.

❖ Cook, uncovered, on HIGH (100%) until the mixture boils, then continue cooking on MEDIUM (50%) or MEDIUM-LOW (30%) until the pudding is cooked:
Semolina, tapioca, ground rice: 10 minutes
Whole rice: 30-45 minutes.

❖ Stir occasionally during cooking.

CAKES

Cakes cooked in the microwave rise well and their flavour is good. Their texture is slightly pudding-like and they do not brown and crisp (though a combination oven, which browns as well as microwaves, will bake some cakes successfully). Generally, very moist mixtures are suited to microwave cooking, as are recipes in which the fats and sugars are melted together.

Tips for making cakes

❖ Choose circular dishes with vertical sides. Ring moulds produce the most successful cakes, with no chance of the centre remaining uncooked.

❖ When trying a recipe for the first time, choose a deep container – cakes rise considerably during cooking. Half fill it only.

❖ Lightly grease the cooking container. Do not coat it with flour or a disagreeable crust will form on the outside of the cake.

❖ Line the base of the container with non-stick baking paper or greased greaseproof paper, for easy removal of the cake.

❖ When cooking a conventional recipe in the microwave, add extra liquid to the mixture – about 15ml (1 tbsp) per egg. Fruit cakes should have a very soft dropping consistency.

❖ Sugar must be well blended into the mixture – lumps of sugar attract microwaves and burn easily.

❖ Small cakes should be arranged in a circle in the micro-wave, with the centre left free.

❖ Place the dish on a microwave rack to make sure the cake cooks evenly.

❖ Cook sponge-type cakes on HIGH (100%) and fruit cakes on MEDIUM (50%) or MEDIUM-LOW (30%). Check with your oven manufacturer's instruction book too.

❖ Stop cooking when the surface of the cake is still slightly moist but the mixture beneath it is cooked. The surface will dry out as it stands.

❖ Allow a standing time before turning the cake out – 5 minutes for sponge-type cakes and 20 minutes for fruit cakes.

❖ Turn the cake out on to a cooling rack lined with non-stick baking paper – to prevent it sticking to the rack.

9

Recipes

TUNA AND TOMATO PASTA

Serves 4 as a starter   *Cooking: 23 mins on* HIGH *(100%)*

1 medium onion, finely chopped
2 garlic cloves, crushed
400g can chopped tomatoes
150ml/¼ pt dry white vermouth
1 vegetable stock cube
175g/6 oz pasta shapes, such as twists or shells
198g can tuna in brine or oil, drained and flaked
30ml/2 tbsp chopped fresh herbs, such as basil, oregano or fennel

1. Put the onion and garlic into a medium bowl, cover and cook for 3 minutes.

2. Stir in the tomatoes, vermouth and crumbled stock cube. Cover and cook for 10 minutes, stirring occasionally.

3. Put the pasta in a large bowl and cover well with boiling water. Cook, uncovered, for 7 minutes, stirring once or twice. Allow to stand for 5 minutes.

4. Meanwhile, add the tuna and herbs to the tomato sauce, cover and cook for 2-3 minutes until hot.

5. Drain the pasta well and serve it topped with the sauce.

WHITE SAUCE

Serves 4-6   *Cooking: 7 minutes on HIGH (100%)*

40g/1½ oz butter
40g/1½ oz flour
600ml/1 pint milk
salt and pepper

1. Put the butter in a bowl or jug. Cook for 1 minute until melted.

2. Stir in the flour, then gradually blend in the milk. Season to taste.

3. Cook, uncovered, for 5-6 minutes, whisking frequently.

CHEESE SAUCE
Add 75-100g/3-4 oz grated cheese to the cooked sauce. Stir until melted.

MUSHROOM SAUCE
At stage 1, add 100g/4 oz finely sliced or chopped mushrooms to the butter, cover and cook for 2 minutes.

MUSTARD SAUCE
Add 2 tbsp ready-made mustard to the cooked sauce.

ONION SAUCE
At stage 1, add a finely chopped onion to the butter, cover and cook for 3 minutes.

PARSLEY SAUCE
Add 2-3 tbsp chopped parsley to the cooked sauce.

PRAWN SAUCE
Add 100g/4 oz small peeled prawns and 1 tbsp lemon juice to the cooked sauce. Cook for 1 minute.

FRESH TOMATO SOUP

Serves 4-6   *Cooking: 25 minutes on HIGH (100%)*

25g/1 oz butter
1 bacon rasher, rind removed and finely chopped
1 medium onion, finely chopped
1 carrot, finely chopped
2 tsp sugar
450g/1 lb fresh tomatoes, chopped, or 400g can chopped
    tomatoes
450ml/¾ pint boiling chicken stock
salt and pepper
bouquet garni
2 tsp lemon juice
2 tbsp tomato purée
chopped parsley to serve
croûtons or crusty bread, to serve

1. Put the butter, bacon, onion, carrot and sugar in a large
    bowl. Cover and cook for 5 minutes.

2. Add the remaining ingredients. Cover and cook for 20
    minutes, stirring occasionally.

3. Allow the soup to stand for 10 minutes then remove the
    bouquet garni.

4. Purée the soup in a blender or food processor. (For a
    really smooth soup, strain through a sieve after
    puréeing.)

5. Reheat if necessary. Sprinkle with chopped parsley and
    serve with croûtons or crusty bread.

CREAM OF TOMATO SOUP

Follow the method above and stir in 150ml/¼ pint single or
double cream before serving.

FISH WITH SUMMER DRESSING

Serves 4   *Cooking: 8 minutes on HIGH (100%)*

4 fillets of white fish, such as cod or haddock, each weighing
   about 175g/6 oz
2 tsp lemon juice or white wine vinegar
150g/5 oz Greek yoghurt
½ tsp concentrated mint sauce
10cm/4 in piece of cucumber, skinned, seeds removed and
   diced
50g/2 oz seedless green grapes, halved
salt and pepper
thin cucumber slices to garnish

1. Arrange the fish fillets in a shallow dish and sprinkle
    with the lemon juice or vinegar. Cover and cook for 5
    minutes.

2. Mix together the yoghurt, mint sauce and cucumber.
    Reserve some grapes for garnish, then stir the remainder
    into the yoghurt mixture. Season lightly with salt and
    pepper. Spread evenly over the fish.

3. Cook for a further 3 minutes or until the fish is just
    cooked. Allow to stand for 2-3 minutes. Serve, garnished
    with cucumber slices and the reserved grapes.

FISH AND BUTTER BEAN CASSEROLE

Serves 4   *Cooking: 16 minutes on HIGH (100%)*

25g/1 oz butter
1 bunch spring onions, chopped
2 tbsp flour
150ml/¼ pint vegetable or fish stock
300ml/½ pint milk
4 tbsp dry white wine
2 tbsp chopped fresh parsley
450g/1 lb white fish, such as cod, haddock, whiting or plaice, skinned and boned
450g/1 lb smoked fish, such as haddock or cod, skinned and boned
415g can butter beans, drained
salt and pepper

1. Put the butter and onions in a large casserole dish, cover and cook for 2 minutes.

2. Stir in the flour then gradually stir in the stock and milk. Cook for 5 minutes, stirring frequently, until boiling.

3. Add the wine and parsley. Cut the fish into chunks and add to the casserole. Stir in the butter beans and season to taste.

4. Cover and cook for 10 minutes, stirring gently once or twice, until the fish is cooked. Serve immediately.

BEEF WITH GINGER AND SPRING ONIONS

Serves 2

Cooking: 6 minutes on HIGH *(100%) plus marinating*

350g/12 oz fillet steak
1 tbsp finely grated fresh root ginger
1 garlic clove, crushed
4 tbsp dry sherry
4 tbsp light soy sauce
1 tsp clear honey
2 tsp oil
4 tsp cornflour
1 bunch spring onions, thickly sliced
cooked rice to serve

1. Cut the steak into thin strips across the grain and put
    into a bowl. Mix together the ginger, garlic, sherry, soy
    sauce and honey. Pour the mixture over the steak,
    stirring to coat it well. Cover and marinate in a cool
    place for 1 hour or more.

2. Put the oil into a large bowl. Use a slotted spoon to lift
    the steak out of its marinade and stir the steak into the
    oil. Cook, uncovered for 2 minutes, or until the steak is
    just cooked, stirring once.

3. Whisk the cornflour into the marinade and pour over
    the steak.

4. Add the onions and cook, uncovered, for 3-4 minutes,
    stirring frequently, until the sauce thickens and boils.
    Serve with rice.

LAMB KORMA

Serves 4

Cooking: 8 minutes on HIGH *(100%) and*
20 minutes on MEDIUM *(50%)*

100g/4 oz ground almonds
2 tbsp mild curry paste
2 tsp oil
1 medium onion, finely chopped
700g/1½ lb fillet or leg of lamb, cubed
75ml/3 fl oz thick natural yoghurt
salt and pepper
75ml/3 fl oz double cream
lemon wedges, to serve

1. Mix the almonds and curry paste with 150ml/¼ pint
    water to make a smooth paste.

2. Put the oil and onion in a large bowl, cover and cook
    for 3 minutes.

3. Add the lamb and stir in the nut paste and yoghurt.
    Season with salt and pepper.

4. Cover and cook for 5 minutes, stirring once or twice.
    Continue cooking, covered, on MEDIUM (50%) for 20
    minutes, stirring occasionally, until the lamb is tender.

5. Stir in the cream and serve with lemon wedges.

PORK IN SWEET AND SOUR SAUCE

Serves 4   *Cooking: 17 minutes on* HIGH *(100%)*

227g can pineapple cubes in fruit juice
chicken or vegetable stock
1 tsp oil
1 medium onion, finely sliced
1 garlic clove, crushed
2 celery sticks, finely sliced
450g/1 lb lean pork, finely sliced
2 tbsp tomato purée
3 tbsp red wine vinegar
3 tbsp soy sauce
3 tbsp brown sugar
2 tbsp cornflour
salt and pepper
1 green pepper, seeded and finely sliced

1. Drain the pineapple and make up the juice to 300ml/ ½ pint with chicken or vegetable stock.

2. Put the oil, onion, garlic and celery in a large bowl. Cover and cook for 5 minutes, stirring once.

3. Stir in the pork and the pineapple-juice mixture.

4. Whisk together the tomato purée, vinegar, soy sauce, sugar and cornflour, then stir into the pork mixture. Season with salt and pepper.

5. Cover and cook for 5 minutes, stirring once, or until boiling. Continue cooking, covered, for 5 minutes, stirring twice, or until the pork is tender.

6. Stir in the pepper and pineapple, cover and cook for 2 minutes until hot.

VEGETABLES IN CREAM SAUCE

Serves 2 as a main meal, 4 as an accompaniment

Cooking: 10 minutes on HIGH *(100%)*

25g/1 oz butter
1 large onion, thinly sliced
4 medium carrots, thinly sliced
4 celery sticks, thinly sliced
225g/8 oz small broccoli florets
100g/4 oz button mushrooms
150ml/¼ pint vegetable stock
1 tbsp cornflour
150ml/¼ pint soured cream
salt and freshly ground black pepper
1 tbsp chopped fresh chives
50g/2 oz toasted cashew nuts or pine nuts

1. Put the butter and onion in a large bowl, cover and cook for 3 minutes.

2. Stir in the carrots, celery, broccoli, mushrooms and stock. Cover and cook for about 8 minutes, stirring occasionally, until the vegetables are just tender.

3. Mix the cornflour with the cream to make a smooth paste, season to taste and add the chives. Stir into the vegetables. Cook, uncovered, for about 2 minutes, stirring once, until the sauce thickens and boils.

4. Scatter the nuts over the top and serve immediately.

WHITE CHOCOLATE MOUSSE

Serves 4-6

Cooking: 4 minutes on MEDIUM-LOW *(30%) and*
45 seconds on HIGH *(100%)*

175g/6 oz white chocolate
1 tbsp clear honey
1 tsp gelatine
150ml/¼ pint whipping cream
2 egg whites
pinch salt
25g/1 oz white or plain chocolate, to decorate

1. Break the white chocolate into a bowl. Add 3 tbsp water and the honey. Cook on MEDIUM-LOW (30%) for about 4 minutes. Stir well until melted and smooth.

2. Put 3 tbsp water in a small bowl and sprinkle the gelatine over. Allow it to stand for 1 minute. Cook on HIGH (100%) for 30-45 seconds, stirring every 15 seconds, until clear (make sure it does not boil). Stir into the white chocolate.

3. Whip the cream until it stands in soft peaks. Fold it into the chocolate mixture.

4. Using a clean bowl and whisk, whisk the egg whites with the salt until stiff. Fold into the chocolate mixture. Spoon into 4-6 small glasses and chill until set.

5. To decorate, chill the remaining chocolate, then make chocolate shavings by drawing a potato peeler across it. Sprinkle some on to the top of each mousse.

Steaming

10

Introducing Steaming

To steam is to cook food in the steam or the vapour given off by boiling water. It is an easy, clean and economical way to cook and can also be an asset to eating healthily.

As a cooking method it can be traced back as far as Neolithic times, particularly in China where the steamer is one of the oldest cooking utensils. To this day it is still a very popular cooking method in Chinese kitchens, where it is unusual to find an oven. Here in the UK, with the explosion of new cooking appliances and gadgets, steaming did lose a little of its popularity. With all the advantages steaming has to offer, its revival is well-deserved.

After all, steaming is a gentle, moist method of cooking that makes the food tender, retains its shape and texture and preserves its colour, all with little chance of the food over-cooking. Food cooked in the steamer takes slightly longer to cook than if it were boiled – so, with that greater margin for error, it's easier to cook vegetables and fish, in particular, to just the right degree of tenderness without overdoing them.

Most people know that steaming is ideal for cooking vegetables and fish (in school, remember being taught that steamed fish was 'highly suitable' for babies, invalids and the elderly?). But would you associate steaming with chicken, duck, beef, pork, lamb, rice, couscous, eggs and fruit? Yes, steaming is great for all these too!

Steaming is economical, with several foods cooking in the baskets of a steamer on one burner of the hob, or in the tiers of an electric steamer. This makes it ideal for a range of people and situations including:

✓   Students and anyone on a limited budget.

✓   People who mostly cook for one or two, or those who need to cook small portions – perhaps for children or for the elderly – and a whole meal can be cooked in the steamer.

✓   Families and cooking for crowds – for example, several vegetables can be cooked in one steamer.

✓   People who need, or want, to eat food that is easily digestible and low in fat.

✓   Reheating food and keeping food hot for short periods.

There are few problems with flavour transfer from one food to another so, for instance, meat and vegetables can be cooked in the bottom tier while a dessert cooks in the upper tier. The natural flavour of food also remains more intense during steaming than, say, during boiling or poaching when more flavour is leached into the water. Because the food is cooked in a moist, steamy atmosphere, it is not likely to dry out and toughen.

Nutritionally, steaming can be beneficial too. Research has shown that steaming retains more of the water-soluble vitamins that are normally lost in boiling – in particular, Vitamin C. Of course, in steaming (as in boiling) even fewer nutrients are lost if the juices that drip from the food are used in a sauce or gravy. Another obvious health advantage is that steamed food needs little or no fat to keep it moist or to help it to cook.

Whether you're looking for healthy, low-fat cooking or good old-fashioned steamed puddings . . . these are the things that a steamer cooks best.

11

At-a-Glance Guide to Steamers

Steaming works on the principle that steam is allowed to circulate freely around the food and, to accommodate this, steamers have lots of perforations or slats in their layers or tiers.

Steaming stand in a large pan
This is the most basic method and one that is ideal for savoury and sweet puddings. The food cooks in a covered dish that sits on a steaming stand in boiling water in a large lidded pan.

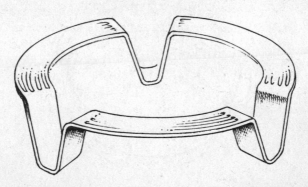

Fig. 6. Steaming stand.

Steaming baskets

This is an inexpensive way to start enjoying the benefits of steaming by cooking a single layer of food. Probably the most useful type is an expanding perforated metal basket that opens out like the petals of a flower. It is placed in or over a saucepan of boiling liquid and covered with a lid that allows enough space for the steam to circulate around the food.

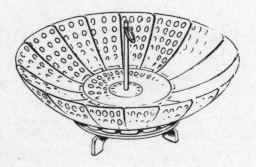

Fig. 7. Steaming basket.

The second type is a static, colander-type affair, usually made of stainless steel, that fits on top of a saucepan. A universal steamer has a stepped base that enables it to be used on pots of various sizes.

Fig. 8. Universal steamer.

The third type is the Chinese-style bamboo steamer that has a slatted base and close-fitting lid and is available in various diameters. Two or three layers can be stacked one on top of the other, ready for steaming over a wok with boiling water in its base.

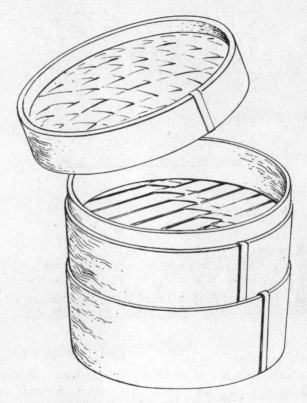

Fig. 9. Bamboo steamer.

Tiered steamers

These are designed for hob use and usually consist of a stainless steel pan with two steaming tiers (or three at the most – more than this and the steam would not be able to cook the food efficiently). Liquid is boiled in the base to produce the steam that cooks the food in the tiers.

Fig. 10. Tiered steamer.

Multi cookers

These, too, are usually stainless steel and are made up of a large pan with a close-fitting, perforated colander that is useful for cooking food in liquid (pasta, for instance). Over this sits a steamer tier, which is then topped with a lid.

Electric steamers

An electric steamer is designed to stand on the kitchen worktop and plug into a 13 amp socket. A timer automatically switches off the steamer at the end of cooking. Two or three heat-resistant plastic tiers sit on the base, which holds the water, and a thermostatically controlled element heats up the water to create the steam. Some models include a drip tray to catch the food juices, a dish for cooking rice and an area with indents in which to cook eggs in their shells.

The advantages of an electric steamer include:

❖ The hob is kept free.

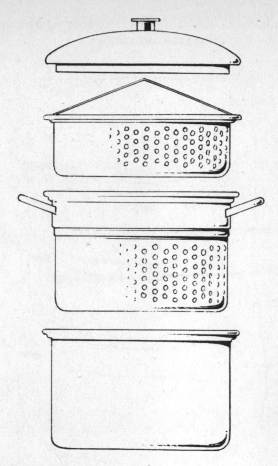

Fig. 11. Multi cooker.

❖   Steam is produced almost instantly.

❖   You can see the food inside.

❖   A whole chicken or a large piece of meat can be cooked in the resulting 'tube' because the bases of the tiers can be removed.

It is worth noting that an electric steamer seems to emit more steam through the vents in the lid (it's helpful to position it near an extractor fan) and therefore needs topping up more frequently during long cooking periods.

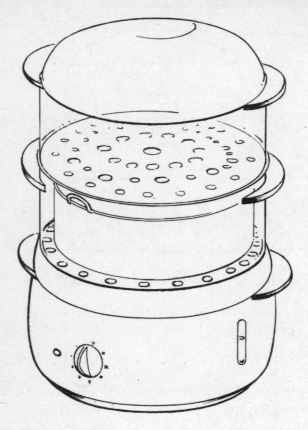

Fig. 12. Electric steamer.

12

How to Get the Best Results

As with any other method of cooking, using fresh, good-quality ingredients will ensure that you get the best results.

❖ Always check that the **lid** fits securely on the steamer, to keep the steam trapped inside the pan and to cook in the shortest time.

❖ The **water** should be heated to a full rolling boil before adding the food to the steamer.

❖ Make sure there is a **gap** of about 2.5cm/1 in between the food and the liquid in the base of the pan. On no account allow the boiling liquid to come into contact with the food (or it will boil and not steam).

❖ Thoroughly **defrost** foods like fish, poultry and meat before steaming. Frozen vegetables can be steamed from frozen.

❖ Choose **equal-size** pieces of food (such as chicken breasts) to encourage even cooking, and cut foods like vegetables into even-sized pieces.

❖ Whenever possible, **arrange** foods in the steamer so that there are gaps between them, to allow the steam to circulate and cook evenly.

❖ Arrange food in an **even layer** in the steamer, again to promote evenly-cooked results. The larger the piece or the thicker the layer of food, the longer the cooking time will be.

❖ Food such as vegetables, fish, meat and poultry can be placed **directly in the steamer**. To prevent food such as steamed puddings becoming too wet, put it in a **covered dish**.

❖ Foods that are likely to **drip**, like fish, poultry and meat, should be placed in the bottom tier, so that they do not affect the other foods.

❖ Put the food with the **shortest cooking time** in the top tier and, if necessary, add it to the steamer at an appropriate stage during cooking. Food in the top tier is further away from the source of the steam and will take slightly longer to cook.

❖ When cooking a **large quantity** of food, it's a good idea to swap the tiers half way through cooking to encourage even cooking.

❖ **Cover** foods only when contact with the steam might cause the dish to spoil – for example, steamed puddings.

❖ For long periods of cooking, such as for a steamed pudding, you may need to **top up** the water in the base of the steamer by adding boiling water from the kettle. To do this with a hob-type steamer, simply lift the tiers off the pan. If you are steaming on a steaming stand in a large pan, simply add the water through the gap between the bowl and pan. Electric steamers usually have a special opening through which you can top up the water – just follow the manufacturer's instructions.

❖ **Resist the temptation** to lift the lid and peek into the steamer during cooking. If you do, steam will be lost and the cooking time will be lengthened.

❖ **Check that food is cooked** before serving. With steaming, as with any other method, cooking times will vary according to the quantity and quality of the food. If the food is not cooked to your liking, simply replace the lid and steam for a few minutes longer.

Quick and simple additions to steamed food
Before steaming, try sprinkling vegetables, fish, poultry or meat with:

➤ Lemon, lime or orange juice, wine vinegar or sherry vinegar.

➤ Finely grated citrus zest – lemon or lime.

➤ Chopped fresh herbs.

➤ Finely chopped or crushed garlic.

➤ Finely chopped fresh root ginger.

➤ Fresh root ginger juice – take a handful of roughly grated root ginger (skin and all) and squeeze tightly so that the delicately-flavoured juice runs from it.

➤ Ground spices (particularly freshly ground) – such as coriander, cumin, chilli, cinnamon, allspice, cloves or nutmeg.

➤ Shallots or mild red or white onion, finely chopped or thinly sliced.

➤ Good quality oil, such as olive, sesame or walnut.

13

Steam Cooking Techniques

These cooking times are provided as a guide only – they will depend on the quantity and quality of the foods to be steamed and, of course, on your personal taste.

EGGS

GUIDE TO STEAMING TIMES		
Quantity: 1-6	Steaming Time	Comments
Whole, in shells: Soft 'boiled' Hard 'boiled'	8-10 minutes 10-18 minutes	The short cooking times are for 1 egg, the longer times are for 6 eggs.
In small dish or ramekin: Soft Hard	5-10 minutes 10-15 minutes	The short cooking times are for 1 egg, the longer times are for 6 eggs.

VEGETABLES

Frozen vegetables need not be defrosted before steaming. Just allow a few minutes longer cooking time.

Avoid strong-flavoured vegetables such as kale or mustard greens – they are likely to transfer their flavour to other foods.

GUIDE TO STEAMING TIMES

Quantity: about 250g/9 oz	Steaming Time	Comments
Artichokes – Globe	30-45 minutes or until the base is tender.	Before cooking, cut off the base so the artichoke sits level in the steamer.
Artichokes – Jerusalem, whole	About 20 minutes	For the best flavour, leave the skins on during steaming (prick them first).
Asparagus	10-15 minutes	Arrange the stalks so that they cross over each other – to allow the steam to circulate. Take care not to overcook or the quick-cooking tips will be too soft.
Beans – Green	10-15 minutes	Arrange the beans so that they cross over each other – to allow the steam to circulate.
Beans – Runner, sliced	10-15 minutes	
Broccoli	10-15 minutes	
Brussels Sprouts	15-20 minutes	Once cooked, try mashing them with a knob of butter and a good grating of fresh nutmeg.

GUIDE TO STEAMING TIMES

Quantity: about 250g/9 oz	Steaming Time	Comments
Cabbage – Quartered Sliced or shredded	About 40 minutes About 15 minutes	
Carrots – Sliced or cut into matchsticks Whole	About 20 minutes 30-45 minutes	
Cauliflower florets	10-15 minutes	
Celeriac, cut into cubes or slices	About 20 minutes	Sprinkling the uncooked celeriac with a little lemon juice helps to keep its colour.
Chinese Leaves, roughly chopped	About 2 minutes	Once cooked, toss with a little soy or oyster sauce.
Corn – Dwarf	About 10 minutes	
Corn on the cob	About 30 minutes	Season with salt after cooking or the skins will toughen.
Courgettes – Small whole Sliced	5-10 minutes About 5 minutes	Take care not to overcook them or they will become watery.
Garlic – Whole cloves	About 10 minutes	Once cooked, squeeze the garlic out of its paper-like casing.

GUIDE TO STEAMING TIMES

Quantity: about 250g/9 oz	Steaming Time	Comments
Garlic – wild	5-10 minutes	For leaves that are just wilted, cook for a very short time.
Leeks, small whole or sliced	20-25 minutes	
Mange Tout	5-10 minutes	Cook until they still have a slight 'bite'.
Mushrooms	About 5 minutes	
Onions – Small whole Sliced	15-20 minutes 10-15 minutes	
Pak Choi, roughly chopped	About 2 minutes	Once cooked, toss with a little soy or oyster sauce.
Parsnip, sliced or cut into cubes	30-45 minutes	Once cooked, leave whole or mash until smooth.
Peas, fresh	8-12 minutes	
Peppers, seeds removed and cut into wide strips	About 10 minutes	
Potatoes, small whole or cut into cubes	About 20 minutes	
Seakale, shredded	20-25 minutes	
Spinach	5-10 minutes	For leaves that are just wilted, cook for a very short time.

GUIDE TO STEAMING TIMES		
Quantity: about 250g/9 oz	**Steaming Time**	**Comments**
Squash, seeds removed and cut into wedges or peeled and cut into cubes	20-30 minutes	Once cooked, serve just as it is or mash until smooth and stir in some cream and ground cinnamon or nutmeg.
Swede, sliced or cubed	30-45 minutes	Once cooked, leave whole or mash until smooth.

COUSCOUS, BULGAR AND RICE

The liquid used could be water or stock with some wine or fruit juice. Put the couscous, bulgar or rice into a container with the liquid and steam uncovered.

GUIDE TO STEAMING TIMES		
Grain	**Quantity**	**Steaming Time**
Couscous	200g/7 oz + 400ml/14 fl oz liquid	10 minutes
Bulgar (or cracked) wheat	200g/7 oz + 400ml/14 fl oz liquid	20-25 minutes
Rice – Long grain white *Brown*	200g/7 oz + 400ml/14 fl oz liquid 200g/7 fl oz + 450ml/16 fl oz liquid	About 25 minutes About 35 minutes

FISH

Frozen fish need not be thawed before steaming but will probably take longer to cook.

GUIDE TO STEAMING TIMES

250-500g/ 9 oz-1 lb 2 oz	Steaming Time	Comments
Thin fillets: cod, haddock, plaice, sole, salmon, etc.	5-10 minutes	Placing them on baking paper makes them easier to remove from the steamer.
Thick fillets or steaks: cod, haddock, monkfish, salmon, tuna, swordfish, etc.	10-15 minutes	
Whole fish: bass, mullet, red snapper, salmon trout, trout, etc.	15-20 minutes	Placing the fish on baking paper makes for easy removal from the steamer.
Clams, cockles	About 5 minutes, until the shells have opened.	Stir half way. Once cooked, discard any unopened shells.
Lobster tails – Fresh Frozen	About 15 minutes About 20 minutes	
Mussels	5-10 minutes or until the shells have opened.	Stir half way. Once cooked, discard any unopened shells.
Oysters, in shells	About 5 minutes, until the shells open easily.	

GUIDE TO STEAMING TIMES		
250-500g/ 9 oz-1 lb 2 oz	**Steaming Time**	**Comments**
Prawns	About 5 minutes, until raw prawns turn pink or cooked prawns are just hot.	Stir half way.
Scallops	About 5 minutes, until just set.	Re-arrange half way.

POULTRY AND MEAT
Thoroughly defrost all poultry and meat before cooking.

GUIDE TO STEAMING TIMES		
Type	**Steaming Time**	**Comments**
Chicken – Boneless breasts	12-15 minutes	The juices should run clear (not pink) when the thickest part of the chicken is pierced with a skewer.
Joints	About 30 minutes	
Duck breasts	25-30 minutes	The skin can be removed before cooking.
Lamb neck fillet, cut in 1cm/½ in slices	About 15 minutes	
Pork fillet, cut in 1cm/½ in slices	About 15 minutes	
Frankfurters and smoked sausages	10-15 minutes	Prick before steaming.

FRUIT

To catch the juices from the fruit, line the steamer with a sheet of baking paper or foil.

GUIDE TO STEAMING TIMES		
Fruit	Steaming Time	Comments
Apples – Whole, peeled Cored and quartered	About 20 minutes About 10 minutes	Rub a little lemon juice over the cut surface.
Apricots – Whole or halved	5-10 minutes	Prick whole apricots before steaming.
Bananas	12-15 minutes, until the skins are brown and just beginning to split open.	
Nectarines – whole or halved	15-20 minutes	Prick whole nectarines before steaming.
Peaches – whole or halved	15-20 minutes	Prick whole peaches before steaming.
Pears – ripe, whole, peeled	About 20 minutes	Rub a little lemon juice over the cut surface.
Plums – whole or halved	5-10 minutes	Prick whole plums before steaming.
Rhubarb, cut into 2.5cm/1 in lengths	5-10 minutes	

14

Recipes

EGGS IN DISHES WITH CREAM AND HERBS

Serves 2   *15 minutes*

This is a quick and easy lunch dish or starter, ideal for serving with crisp fingers of toast.

butter
2 eggs
salt and freshly ground black pepper
2 tbsp double or soured cream
1 tbsp chopped fresh herbs, such as parsley or coriander
paprika

1.   Lightly butter two small dishes or ramekins and crack an egg into each. Season with salt and pepper and spoon the cream over the top. Sprinkle with the herbs and a little paprika.

2.   Put the dishes in the steamer and cover with the lid. Steam for 6-10 minutes or until the eggs are set to your taste.

EGGS WITH PANCETTA

Make the recipe above, first lining the dishes with wafer-thin slices of pancetta or Parma ham.

CORN ON THE COB WITH ONION AND HERB BUTTER

Serves 2   *30 minutes + preparation*

This easy lunch dish works well with frozen corn too.

2 corn on the cob, husks removed
50g/1¾ oz soft butter
4 spring onions, chopped
1 tbsp finely chopped fresh parsley
leaves from 1 fresh rosemary sprig
salt and freshly ground black pepper

1. Put the corn in the bottom tier of the steamer and cover with the lid. Steam for 15 minutes.

2. Meanwhile, put the butter into a bowl that will fit into the steamer. Add the onions, parsley and rosemary leaves. Season lightly with salt and pepper. Cover the dish with foil, crimping the edges securely to the sides of the dish.

3. Put the dish in the second tier, add it to the steamer and cover with the lid. Steam for a further 15 minutes or until the corn is tender.

4. To serve, season the corn with salt and pepper to taste, stir the buttery juices and pour over the corn.

SQUASH PARCELS WITH BROWN SUGAR
AND CINNAMON

Serves 4   *30 minutes + preparation*

Squash cooks beautifully in the steamer. Delicious juices collect in these parcels – mash the squash into them as you eat. (Try with other types of squash too!) Serve with grilled meat or fish, or just as it is with freshly grated Parmesan.

1 small acorn squash
4 tsp muscovado sugar
½ tsp ground cinnamon
100g/3½ oz butter
4 tsp lemon juice or white wine, cider or sherry vinegar
**2 tbsp finely chopped fresh herb, such as parsley, basil or
  coriander**
salt and freshly ground black pepper

1.   Cut the squash into quarters and scoop out and discard the seeds and membranes. Remove the skin and cut into bite-size cubes.

2.   Divide the squash (in even layers) between four squares of foil or baking paper, each large enough to enclose it completely. Mix together the sugar and cinnamon and sprinkle over the squash. Top each with one quarter of the butter, lemon juice, herb and seasoning. Close the parcels, securing the seams well.

3.   Put the parcels in the steamer and cover with the lid. Steam for about 30 minutes or until the squash is soft and tender.

BULGAR WHEAT WITH HERBS AND LEMON

Serves 4-6   *25 minutes + preparation*

2 tbsp olive oil
250g/9 oz bulgar or cracked wheat
1 medium red onion, finely chopped
500ml/18 fl oz hot vegetable stock
1 tbsp finely chopped fresh mint or 1 tsp dried
1 tbsp finely chopped fresh oregano or thyme leaves, or 1 tsp
** dried**
25g/1 oz sultanas
1 lemon
salt and freshly ground black pepper

1. Put the oil into a bowl that will fit in the steamer. Stir in the bulgar wheat and onion. Pour over the hot stock, add the herbs and sultanas and stir well. Leave to stand for 10 minutes.

2. Finely grate the rind and squeeze the juice from half the lemon (reserve the other half for serving). Add rind and juice to the bulgar wheat and season with salt and pepper.

3. Put the uncovered bowl into the steamer and cover with the lid. Steam for 20-25 minutes or until the bulgar wheat is tender, stirring half way.

4. Tip into a large, warm serving bowl and fluff up with a fork. Cut the reserved lemon into wedges and arrange on top.

Tip: Serve as an accompaniment to lamb or as part of a buffet.

PLAICE ROLLS WITH LEMON AND
SPRING ONIONS

Serves 4   *8 minutes + preparation*

Choose plaice fillets that have had black (rather than white) skin removed – they will be thicker. This recipe is also good when made with lemon or Dover sole. Serve with fresh steamed vegetables or a mixed salad.

1 lemon, scrubbed
25g/1 oz butter
85g/3 oz fresh breadcrumbs
3 spring onions, finely chopped
salt and freshly ground black pepper
8 plaice fillets

1.   Finely grate the rind off half the lemon and squeeze 1 tablespoonful of juice from the same half.

2.   Melt the butter and stir in the lemon rind and 1 table-spoonful of juice. Add the breadcrumbs, onions and seasoning and stir lightly until well mixed.

3.   Spread the breadcrumb mixture over the skinned sides of the plaice and roll up each one.

4.   Arrange in the steamer and cover with the lid. Steam for 6-8 minutes until just cooked through.

SEAFOOD PARCELS

Serves 2   *15 minutes + preparation*

This recipe uses white fish, mussels and prawns but vary the seafood to suit yourself. Buy a small amount of several types of fish – such as salmon, monkfish, tuna, clams, oysters and cockles. Serve with fresh bread.

50g/1¾ oz soft butter
1 small garlic clove, crushed
1 tsp finely chopped fresh parsley
freshly ground black pepper
225g/8 oz raw prawns in their shells, heads and legs removed
225g/8 oz raw mussels in their shells, scrubbed
2 tbsp dry white wine or vermouth
2 tbsp double cream
lemon wedges, to serve

1.   With a fork, blend together the butter, garlic, parsley and pepper.

2.   Divide the prawns and mussels between two large squares of thick (or double) foil, gathering up the sides. Into each parcel spoon half the wine and half the cream. Top with half the butter mixture. Seal the foil tightly, leaving plenty of room inside for the mussels to open.

3.   Put the parcels into one or, preferably, two steamer tiers and cover with the lid. Steam for about 10-15 minutes or until the mussels have opened and the prawns are pink.

4.   Serve with the lemon wedges for squeezing over.

CHICKEN IN A PACKET WITH TARRAGON AND CREAM SAUCE

Serves 2   *20 minutes + preparation*

There's lots of sauce, so serve this with crusty bread or rice (steamed above or below the chicken). To serve, simply tear open a foil parcel and allow the contents to slide out on to a warm serving plate.

2 boneless chicken breasts, skin removed
salt and freshly ground black pepper
1½ tbsp chopped fresh tarragon or 1 tsp dried
1 small leek, thinly sliced
1 small carrot, cut into thin matchsticks
4 tsp vermouth or dry white wine
4 tsp double cream

1. Season the chicken breasts lightly with salt and pepper, then put each one on to a piece of foil, large enough to enclose it completely. Sprinkle the tarragon over the chicken. Pile the leek and carrot on top, then spoon over the vermouth and cream. Season the vegetables lightly with salt and pepper.

2. Close the parcels, securing the edges.

3. Put the parcels in the steamer and cover with the lid. Steam for 15-20 minutes until the chicken is cooked through (the juices should run clear when the chicken is pierced with the point of a sharp knife).

PORK IN FOIL – GREEK STYLE

Serves 2   *30 minutes + preparation*

This recipe is based on Stifado, a dish enjoyed in Crete. There it is cooked in the oven. The special background flavour comes from the allspice – if you don't have any to hand, use ground cloves instead.

1 tbsp olive oil, plus extra for brushing
1 small red onion, thinly sliced
300g/10½ oz pork tenderloin, cut diagonally into 1cm/½ in thick slices
salt and freshly ground black pepper
1 garlic clove, finely chopped
2 medium tomatoes, sliced
2 pinches of ground allspice
4 generous sprigs of thyme
2 tsp red wine vinegar

1. Lightly brush two large squares of foil with oil. On each piece, lay half the onion and half the pork. Season with salt and pepper, scatter the garlic over and add the tomato slices. Sprinkle with allspice, add the thyme sprigs and drizzle over the oil and vinegar.

2. Seal the parcels, securing the edges well. Arrange them in the steamer and cover with the lid.

3. Steam for about 30 minutes until cooked through.

LAMB WITH LEEKS, HONEY AND LEMON

Serves 2   *15 minutes + preparation*

This is a delicious combination of flavours and a lovely pool of sweet juices collects around the lamb as it cooks. Don't be tempted to omit the parsley and lemon topping – it makes all the difference.

1 garlic clove, crushed
1 tbsp clear honey
finely grated rind and juice of ½ a lemon
salt and freshly ground black pepper
350g/12 oz lean lamb neck fillet, cut into 1cm/½ in slices
2 small leeks, sliced
2 tbsp finely chopped fresh parsley

1. Put the garlic and honey into a bowl. Blend in the lemon juice and seasoning. Add the lamb slices and toss until coated. Cover and leave to stand for about 30 minutes (or up to 2 hours).

2. Line the bottom steamer tier with baking paper and arrange the lamb in an even layer on top.

3. Put the leeks into the second tier.

4. Assemble the steamer and cover with the lid. Steam for about 15 minutes until the lamb is cooked.

5. Meanwhile, mix together the lemon rind and parsley.

6. To serve, pile the leeks on to warm serving plates and arrange the lamb on top. Spoon over the juices that have collected on the paper and sprinkle the lemon and parsley over the top.

PECAN AND MAPLE SYRUP PUDDING

Serves 6   *2 hours + preparation*

Pecan nuts and maple syrup make a heavenly partnership! Use real maple syrup if you can, not the 'flavoured' variety of syrup. Serve each portion topped with a spoonful of Greek yoghurt or crème fraîche.

3 tbsp maple syrup
50g/1¾ oz pecan halves
115g/4 oz soft butter
115g/4 oz golden caster sugar
2 medium eggs, lightly beaten
1 tbsp milk
115g/4 oz self-raising flour
1 tsp baking powder

1. Lightly butter a 1.2 litre/2 pint pudding basin and put a small disc of baking paper in the bottom.

2. Spoon the maple syrup into the basin. Arrange half the pecan halves in the syrup. Finely chop the rest.

3. Put the butter, sugar, eggs and milk into a mixing bowl and sift over the flour and baking powder. Beat well until smooth, then stir in the chopped nuts. Spoon mixture into basin and level the surface.

4. Cover with baking paper and then with a large piece of foil. Gather up the edges, crimping them securely against the sides of the basin.

5. Put into the steamer and cover with the lid. Steam for 2 hours, topping up the boiling water as necessary.

COCONUT CREAMS WITH MANGO

Serves 4   *10 minutes + preparation*

Serve with dainty crisp biscuits, such as amaretti – it's a good idea to crumble one on top of each serving.

200ml carton coconut cream
200ml double cream
finely grated rind of 1 lime or lemon
50g/1¾ oz caster sugar
4 medium eggs, beaten
1 large ripe mango, peeled, stone removed and chopped

1. Pour the coconut cream and double cream into a small saucepan, add the lime rind and sugar and heat gently, stirring, until the sugar has dissolved (alternatively, heat in the microwave for about 2 minutes, stirring once or twice). Leave to cool slightly.

2. Lightly whisk the eggs, then whisk in the coconut mixture. Pour into four small dishes or ramekins.

3. Put the uncovered dishes in the steamer and cover with the lid. Steam for about 10 minutes or until the custards are just set.

4. Leave to cool, then chill for 1-2 hours.

5. Serve topped with the fresh mango.

Blending
and
Processing

15

Blending

Though the blender has been around for well over half a century, it has often taken a back seat to the more glamorous food processor. However, it is a mistake to think that one can replace the other. There are indeed some tasks that the two appliances do equally well, but a blender can create a smoothness that no food processor can match. Today, with health high on everyone's schedule, the blender really comes into its own for whizzing up your favourite smoothies and fruit drinks, vegetable and fruit purées, dips, dressings, sauces and soups. And unlike a food processor, a blender copes well with small quantities, so it's particularly good at preparing baby food.

Blenders (sometimes referred to as liquidisers) are available as self-contained, free-standing units or as an attachment to a table-top food mixer or multi-purpose kitchen machine. The former will have its own power base with motor, while the latter will use the motor of the food mixer or kitchen machine. Short, sharp, stainless steel blades rotate at high speed, cutting through the food that is in contact with them and forcing the mixture up the sides of the jar and then down the centre (like a whirlpool action), back on to the blades in surges.

What they are capable of doing depends mainly on the power of the motor. The more powerful models (350 watts and over) will handle most tasks, including chopping, mixing, puréeing, liquefying and, often, crushing ice and grinding coffee. Some blenders are sold with their own accessory blade or attachment for ice crushing or coffee grinding.

Because the blender jars are tall and narrow and because the blades are small and rotate so fast, air cannot be incorporated into the food. So a blender will not 'whip' or 'whisk' foods such as egg whites or cream. However, when it comes to making purées, sauces, soups and drinks, a blender is the best tool for the job.

What to look for

❖ Look for a sturdy, heavy base with non-slip feet – to keep the blender from wobbling or 'walking' across the worktop when operating at high speeds or handling heavy jobs such as crushing ice.

❖ On top of the base sits a heat (and cold) resistant jar made of toughened glass, heavy plastic or stainless steel. Glass jars are sturdy though they can be quite heavy and can break or crack if dropped. Plastic jars are lighter and very tough but they can get scratched or discoloured. The main advantage of both glass and plastic is that the contents of the jar are visible. Stainless steel is probably the most durable – it copes with very hot food and keeps frozen drinks icy cold, but you cannot see what's going on inside it without removing the lid.

❖ The size and shape of jar varies from model to model. Look for a wide opening for easy filling, easy-to-read measurement markings on the side of the jar and a shape that is easy to scrape out. A handle and large spout make for ease of use and pouring.

❖ Make sure the lid fits tightly in the top of the jar.

❖ Most models include a small twist-lock plug in the centre of the lid that can be removed to release steam or to add ingredients while the machine is running (and without splattering the kitchen). These plugs often double as small measuring cups.

❖ Make sure the blades can be removed for easy cleaning, with a rubber gasket to provide a tight seal that prevents liquids from leaking out from the jar on to the base.

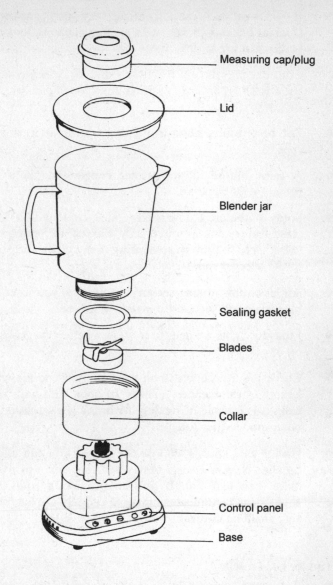

Measuring cap/plug

Lid

Blender jar

Sealing gasket

Blades

Collar

Control panel

Base

Fig 13. A typical blender.

❖ If you want to be able to blend very small quantities (such as one or two egg yolks for mayonnaise), look for blades that are set low in the jar.

❖ Controls may be push-button, dial or touch-control pads. Each type is easy to use though touch pads are the easiest to clean.

❖ For best results, choose a blender with at least two speeds.

❖ A pulse button allows greater control and helps to prevent over blending.

❖ Some of the more advanced models come with a 'step start' feature that automatically starts the blender at a lower speed to prevent splattering then quickly increases to the selected speed.

❖ An 'electronic mixing sensor' automatically adjusts the blender speed when more power is needed.

❖ Indicator lights are helpful to show whether the power is on or off.

❖ Check the instruction book before buying, to see what quantities the blender is likely to cope with and what tasks it is capable of dealing with. It's always useful to have some recipes too.

❖ Having said all this, choose the largest you can afford because blenders work best when they are not much more than half full. If you enjoy making your own soup, it can be time consuming and fiddly to blend it in very small quantities.

Tips for good results
❖ Cut, break or tear large items of food into smaller pieces. About 2.5-3.5cm/1-1½ in is ideal.

❖ To work efficiently, there must be enough food to cover the blades and, except when chopping small amounts of dry foods, it's best to add a small amount of liquid to make sure that the food at the top becomes incorporated and gets blended.

❖ Unless a recipe states otherwise, always put liquid ingredients into the blender first followed by the dry ingredients.

❖ Do not overfill the blender – a maximum of half full is a general guide but do check with your instruction book to make sure.

❖ Fit the lid securely on to the jar before turning on the blender.

❖ The speed you choose will depend on the type of food that is to be blended. If in doubt, start on a low speed and, if little happens, increase the speed. Whenever possible, be guided by your manufacturer's instruction book.

❖ When blending hot foods or liquids, such as soups and sauces, remove the cap in the lid and place a thick cloth over the top. This allows the steam to escape instead of forcing the lid up and causing the hot contents to spill out. Always start blending on a low speed and gradually increase it. At the risk of stating the obvious, please do not place your bare hand over the blender lid.

❖ To add extra ingredients while the machine is running, use low-to-medium speed, remove the cap and feed items or drizzle in liquid through the hole.

❖ Avoid over-processing foods. A blender works incredibly fast (so don't be tempted to walk away from it while the motor is running). Stop and check the consistency every few seconds, scraping down the sides of the jar if necessary.

❖ Use a rubber spatula to scrape down the sides and to remove food from the blender jar.

❖ Always make sure the blender is switched off before inserting any utensil into the blender. Never put a utensil (or your fingers!) anywhere near the blades while the blender jar is still sitting on its base.

❖   Always switch off the blades and make sure the motor is completely stopped before lifting the blender jar off its base.

❖   Clean your blender jar quickly and easily by adding warm water (up to half full) and a drop of washing up liquid and blending on low speed until the sides are clean. Rinse and dry.

❖   For complete cleaning, dismantle and wash and dry pieces separately.

❖   Always switch off and unplug the blender before dismantling it.

❖   The manufacturer's instruction book will indicate which parts of the blender are dishwasher proof.

❖   The power base (containing the motor) should never be immersed in water.

❖   Finally (and it's another obvious point, I know) do not store food in your blender for any length of time. Empty, wash and dry it after each use.

16

Getting the Best From Your Blender

Your blender will quickly and easily undertake all those difficult and/or time-consuming jobs that would otherwise require a great deal of effort. Just remember to scrape down the sides if necessary as you go. Keep your blender on the kitchen worktop ready to:

❖ **Chop vegetables and fruit**, raw or cooked. Put small whole pieces or chopped large pieces into the blender, cover and pulse on low speed until the desired consistency is achieved. Small amounts work best.

❖ **Purée cooked or canned vegetables**. Use medium-high speed, adding a little water or vegetable stock if necessary.

❖ **Purée raw soft fruit**. Blend fruit such as strawberries, raspberries or currants on medium-high speed. The resulting 'sauce' can be sweetened with sugar to taste.

❖ **Purée canned or cooked fruit**. Drain the fruit, reserving the juice. Blend on medium-high speed, adding sufficient juice to make a smooth purée.

❖ **Chop, shred or purée cooked meat**. Cut the meat into small cubes and put into the blender (with a little stock, water or milk if wished). Starting on low speed, pulse

117

until the mixture is as coarse or smooth as you wish, adding extra liquid if necessary.

❖ **Purée cottage or ricotta cheese**. When making dips, spreads, fillings for pasta or cheesecake mixtures, spoon the cheese into the blender (with or without added ingredients) and blend at medium speed, adding a little milk (or liquid from the recipe) if necessary.

❖ **Chop hard cheese**. Cut the cold cheese (such as Parmesan or Cheddar) into cubes, put into the blender and pulse on high speed until very finely chopped. Suitable for up to about 85g/3 oz cheese. Use it as you would grated cheese.

❖ **Chop or grind nuts**. Put the nuts into the blender and pulse on medium-low speed until coarsely or finely chopped or finely ground. It's best to blend nuts in small batches – in a large batch, the nuts at the bottom may have ground to a fine powder before the top ones are chopped.

❖ **Break up seeds**, the ones that are difficult to digest whole (such as linseed and sesame), for adding raw to muesli and other breakfast cereals. Add sufficient to cover the blades of the blender and pulse on high until the seeds are broken.

❖ **Chop herbs** for sauces, casseroles, salads and pesto. Put the washed and dried herbs into the blender and pulse on medium-low speed until finely chopped.

❖ **Chop fresh coconut**. Remove the coconut from its shell and cut into cubes. Put into the blender and pulse on medium speed until it reaches the consistency you want.

❖ **Chop chocolate**. Break the chocolate into the blender and pulse on medium-low until chopped to the required coarseness.

❖ **Make breadcrumbs** for stuffings, bread sauce or breadcrumb coatings. Cut or tear bread into small pieces, put into the blender and pulse on medium-high speed until the crumbs are as coarse or fine as you wish.

❖ **Make biscuit crumbs** for cheesecake bases or dessert toppings. Break large biscuits into pieces, put into the blender and pulse on low speed until the crumbs are as coarse or fine as you need.

❖ **Make cake crumbs for desserts**. Break the cake into pieces, put into the blender and pulse on low speed until the crumbs are formed.

❖ **Grind coffee beans**. Put a small amount into the blender and pulse on high speed until it is ground as fine as you want.

❖ **Prepare baby food**. Blend fruit, vegetables, meat, fish or a mixture of foods from the adults' meal, starting on a low speed, until smooth. If necessary add a little water or milk to get the consistency you desire.

❖ **Mix liquids**. When a recipe calls for liquid ingredients to be whisked or mixed together, pop them into the blender on high speed. This is particularly useful when honey, golden syrup, treacle, marmalade or jam needs to be blended into liquid.

❖ **Purée soups**. Allow the soup to cool slightly before pouring into the blender (you may need to do this in batches). Starting on a low speed, blend until smooth. Take care not to overfill the blender and never start on a high speed as hot liquid may spill out and cause scalds (see page 115).

❖ **Make quick sandwich spreads**, with hard-boiled eggs, cheese, canned beans or left-over pieces of cooked meat or fish. Just whizz them up in the blender with a little soft butter, ricotta or cream cheese.

❖ **Mix bastes and marinades**.

❖ **Make salad dressings**. The blender is excellent at emulsifying salad dressings so that they are less likely to separate on standing. Put your favourite proportions into the blender and blend on high speed until smooth and thickened.

❖ **Mix sauces**. When making a white sauce, put the milk, flour and seasonings into the blender and blend on low speed until smooth. Transfer the mixture and cook in the usual way.

❖ **Mix batter for pancakes and Yorkshire pudding**.

❖ **Remove lumps from gravies and sauces**. If you end up with a lumpy sauce, simply tip it into the blender and, starting on low speed, blend until smooth. Reheat, stirring, and bring it to the boil.

❖ **Reconstitute frozen fruit juice**. Tip the frozen block of fruit concentrate into the blender and add some or all (depending on the capacity of your blender) of the measured water. Blend on medium speed until completely combined.

❖ **Pulp fruit for a healthy juice drink**. Put washed and chopped raw fruit of your choice (oranges, lemons, grapefruit, pears, pineapple, melon) into the blender and, starting on a low speed, pulse until coarsely chopped. Increase the speed and blend until finely chopped. Press the mixture through a sieve to extract the juice.

❖ **Make milk shakes, smoothies and other drinks**.

❖ **Crush ice (in some blenders only)**. Many blenders are capable of crushing ice – check in your instruction book for directions on how to do it. Small ice cubes work best and some models require the addition of a small amount of water.

❖ **Make vanilla sugar**. Put some caster sugar into the blender with a chopped vanilla pod. Blend on high speed until the pod is very finely chopped and dispersed through the sugar. Sieve to remove any large pieces of pod and store the vanilla sugar in an airtight container.

17

Recipes for Blenders

FRESH HERB DIP

Serves 6-8

284ml carton soured cream
200g carton cream cheese
3 spring onions, chopped
small handful of fresh herb leaves such as basil, coriander or
   parsley
salt and freshly milled pepper
milk

1. Put the cream into the blender followed by the cheese, onion, herbs and seasoning. Blend on medium-to-high speed until smooth, scraping down the sides occasionally and thinning with a little milk to make a soft consistency.

2. Adjust the seasoning to taste, cover and chill until required.

3. Serve with vegetable crudités, crisps or crackers.

BEETROOT SOUP WITH SOURED CREAM AND DILL

Serves 6

This simple adaptation of the Ukrainian soup called Borscht is made with ready-cooked beetroot (the type to be found in vacuum packs on the fresh salad counter). Serve it chilled in summer or hot at other times of the year.

2 x 250g packets cooked beetroot
6 spring onions, chopped
400g can chopped tomatoes
1 tbsp clear honey
500ml/18 fl oz good quality vegetable stock
2 tbsp lemon juice
salt and freshly milled black pepper
1 tbsp finely chopped fresh dill
142ml carton soured cream

1. Put the beetroot (with its juice) into the blender with the onions, tomatoes and honey. Blend until smooth (you may need to scrape down the sides occasionally).

2. Tip into a large bowl (for chilled soup) or saucepan (for hot soup) and stir in the stock and the lemon juice. Season to taste with salt and pepper.

3. Either cover and chill until needed or heat gently until just bubbling.

4. Meanwhile, stir the dill into the soured cream.

5. Serve the soup in bowls, each topped with a spoonful of the dill cream.

HAM, CHERRY TOMATO AND THYME TART

Serves 4

20cm/8 in uncooked pastry case
6 thin slices of Italian dry cured ham, or an 80g packet
12-16 cherry tomatoes
3 medium eggs
250g carton fromage frais
1-2 tbsp fresh thyme leaves
salt and freshly ground black pepper
1-2 tbsp finely grated Parmesan cheese

1. Put a baking sheet in the oven while you preheat it to 200°C/400°F/Gas Mark 6.

2. Line a metal flan dish with the pastry and then arrange the ham slices over the base and sides of the pastry, overlapping them and allowing them to stand slightly higher than the pastry sides.

3. Scatter the tomatoes over the top.

4. Put the eggs into the blender, add the fromage frais, thyme and seasoning. Blend until smooth. Pour the mixture over the tomatoes.

5. Put the filled tart on the hot baking sheet in the oven and cook at 200°C/400°F/Gas Mark 6 for about 35 minutes, sprinkling the cheese over the top for the final 10 minutes.

SALMON FRIES

Serves 2

250g/9 oz skinless salmon fillets, cut into 2.5cm/1 in cubes
3 tbsp tartare sauce
2 tbsp chopped fresh dill or parsley
1 tsp finely grated lemon rind (optional)
1 spring onion, chopped
salt and freshly milled black pepper
olive oil for frying

1. Put the salmon into the blender with the tartare sauce, herb, lemon rind, onion and seasoning. Blend (pulse) on medium speed until fairly smooth.

2. Heat a little oil in a frying pan, add spoonfuls of the mixture and fry, turning once, until golden brown and cooked through.

3. Serve immediately with a mixed salad or in split rolls with salad leaves, thin slices of red onion and lemon wedges for squeezing over.

PRAWN SESAME STICKS

Makes about 24

A delicious Chinese-style snack that's ideal for serving with drinks. Use bread that is one or two days old.

1 medium egg
1 tbsp rice wine or dry sherry
225g/8 oz peeled prawns
1 tbsp grated root ginger
2 spring onions, chopped
1 rounded tsp cornflour
small pinch of ground star anise
salt
4 bread slices
4 tbsp sesame seeds
oil for frying

1. Put the egg and rice wine into the blender followed by the prawns, ginger, onions, cornflour, star anise and salt. Blend on medium speed to make a smooth paste, scraping down the sides occasionally.

2. Spread the paste thickly on one side of each bread slice and sprinkle the sesame seeds over.

3. Heat some oil in a deep frying pan and fry the bread, turning once, until crisp and golden brown on both sides. Drain on kitchen paper.

4. Cut each slice into six pieces and serve warm.

MOCHA POTS

Serves 4

150g/5½ oz dark chocolate
1½ tbsp instant coffee granules
1 medium egg
2 tbsp caster sugar
1 tsp vanilla extract
pinch of salt
150ml/¼ pint full cream milk
cocoa powder or icing sugar for dusting

1. Break the chocolate into the blender and buzz briefly until chopped into small pieces.

2. Add the coffee, egg, sugar, vanilla and salt.

3. Bring the milk just to the boil, pour into the blender, cover and blend for about 1 minute until smooth.

4. Pour into small serving dishes (or coffee cups) and chill for several hours.

5. Just before serving, sift a little cocoa or icing sugar over the top of each 'pot' (if you are using coffee cups, sit them on matching saucers and allow some of the powder to stray on to each saucer).

6. Serve with crisp biscuits.

PLUM CLAFOUTIS

Serves 4-6

Here is a French dessert that is traditionally made with whole,
unpitted black cherries. As well as plums, it works well with
peaches and apricots. Serve the pudding warm, dusted with
icing sugar and a jug of cream.

500g/18 oz plums, halved and stones removed
115g/4 oz caster sugar
300ml/½ pint milk
3 medium eggs
125g/4½ oz plain flour
pinch of salt
butter

1. Toss the plums in half the sugar and leave to stand for
    about 30 minutes.

2. Meanwhile, put the milk into the blender followed by
    the eggs, flour, salt and the remaining sugar. Blend on
    high speed until smooth, scraping down the sides if
    necessary.

3. Cover and leave to stand until required, stirring well
    before using.

4. Butter a shallow ovenproof dish, scatter the plums in it
    and pour the batter over.

5. Cook in a preheated oven at 180°C/350°F/Gas Mark 4
    for about 30 minutes or until the batter is cooked
    through.

A BASIC MILK SHAKE

Serves 2

Choose your flavour according to the ice cream.

300ml/½ pint cold milk
142ml carton double cream
4 scoops ice cream, such as vanilla
few drops of vanilla extract

1.   Put all the ingredients into the blender and blend on high speed until smooth.

2.   Serve immediately.

Follow the same basic method for the following flavours:

MOCHA MILK SHAKE

Serve with some drinking chocolate sprinkled over the top.

300ml/½ pint cold milk
4 tbsp double cream
4 scoops chocolate ice cream
1½ tbsp coffee essence

STRAWBERRY AND VANILLA MILK SHAKE

Change the flavour with your choice of soft fruit.

600ml/1 pint milk
115g/4 oz ripe strawberries
4 scoops vanilla ice cream
2 drops vanilla extract

MANGO LASSI

Serves 3-4

Try serving this refreshing yoghurt drink after a dish of curry. Delicious! If your blender is suitable for crushing ice, add a few cubes to the mixture in step 1.

3 ripe mangoes, peeled and stones removed
150g carton natural yoghurt
3 tbsp lime juice
2 tbsp clear honey

1.   Put all the ingredients into the blender.

2.   Blend on high speed until smooth.

3.   Serve immediately.

PEACH COOLER

Serves 2-3

2 ripe peaches, peeled, stones removed, and cut into chunks
2 tbsp clear honey
600ml/1 pint milk, chilled
1 ripe banana

1.   Put the peaches, honey and milk into the blender and break in the banana.

2.   Blend on high speed until smooth.

3.   Serve immediately – in tall glasses with straws!

18

Food Processors

This is cooking for people who don't like to get their hands dirty, which can turn pastry-making from a chore into an easy two-minute operation and bread-making from a complex rite into a fool-proof success every time.

A good food processor can do much of the work of liquidisers and food mixers. All the food is processed in one bowl, whether chopped, mixed, puréed, sliced or grated, using a few attachments which are simple to fit and no problem to store. In addition, you can choose a more sophisticated model which may well include accessories that extend the usage of your food processor. Some models have a separate blender goblet, citrus press, herb and spice mill or juice extractor. As all models vary from brand to brand, please read your manufacturer's handbook carefully so that you understand how your food processor should be used.

BOWL

The bowl is made of a tough, clear plastic so you can watch food as it is processed. Most of the bowls on the market will withstand the addition of liquids at boiling point and many of them may be washed in a dishwasher.

The lid of the bowl is also of clear plastic and incorporates a feed tube through which additional food may be introduced during a processing operation. A plastic pusher fits within the tube and this keeps fingers away from the sharp cutting edges of the attachments. NEVER PUSH FOOD THROUGH THE FEED TUBE USING YOUR FINGERS – ALWAYS USE THE PUSHER PROVIDED. Some pushers are made of clear plastic and are calibrated with metric and imperial quantities for use as a handy measuring cup.

MOTOR

The bowl sits on a central spindle which creates the drive for the attachments. The powerful motor is situated beside the bowl in most food processors, but in a couple of cases the bowl sits on top of the motor, so taking up slightly less space on the work top. The motors vary in power from model to model, and some processors are belt driven while others are driven by an induction motor.

The speed of the motor is the main difference between food processors, and as the number of speeds provided affects the price, you need to appreciate the benefits of multi-speed. The basic models generally operate at only one speed which equates with the fastest speed of the more expensive processors providing a choice of up to 12 speeds. The more advanced models detect which attachment is fitted and adjust the speed automatically to suit the task – slower speeds allow you, for example, to whisk egg whites (with a special attachment) and mix cakes and yeasted mixtures more satisfactorily.

On occasions it is necessary to chop or blend additional food using a pulsing action, a short burst of power which allows you to control the degree of processing. The more sophisticated models are fitted with a pulse button, but with the basic processors you need to do this manually by switching the motor on and off (at the appliance, not at the wall switch). A pulse button is a useful facility as it is so easy to over-process, especially when chopping.

ATTACHMENTS

Steel blade

The universal attachment of all food processors is the steel blade, a very sharp double-bladed knife which sits on the drive spindle and whizzes around at amazing speed to chop, mix, blend and purée. Most recipes require the steel blade for all or part of the operation and in the recipes that follow 'processing' means the use of the steel blade.

Fig. 14. A steel blade.

Take care always to handle this attachment by its plastic stem to avoid cutting yourself. It is best to leave the steel blade fitted onto the drive spindle when the processor isn't in use as storage elsewhere could lead to accidents and blunting of the cutting edges. Some manufacturers provide useful plastic sleeves to protect the blades.

Plastic blade

Not standard on all processors, the plastic blade resembles the steel blade but, instead of two sharp cutting knives, the blunt plastic allows you to mix in without chopping and is recommended for use with bread, pastry and cake mixes. Useful but not essential.

Dough hook

For bread making – the bent prongs are designed to knead the mixture rather than just blend it.

Slicing disc

All models are provided with a slicing disc which fits onto the drive spindle, positioning the cutting disc close to the lid. Food is pushed through the feed tube and as the disc rotates at high speed, the food is sliced and falls into the bottom of the bowl.

The earlier discs had a fixed stem which fitted over the drive spindle. This presented a minor storage problem, soon overcome though by the provision of an ingenious wall rack into which the various discs could be slotted. Some of the later models provide interchangeable discs which can be clipped onto a single plastic stem or disc carrier, a much neater solution.

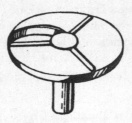

Fig. 15. A slicing disc.

Shredding/grating disc

As with the slicing disc, the shredding/grating disc is a standard accessory and operates in exactly the same way. It is possible to get a slicer and shredder in one disc – you simply reverse the blade on the disc carrier for whichever operation is required. Similarly, it is possible to get a reversible shredder which gives coarse shredding on one side and fine grating on the other. Some manufacturers offer a wide range of grating coarseness, from a very fine Parmesan grater to a coarser shredder to produce juliennes or thicker strips of vegetables.

Fig. 16. A shredding/grating disc.

Chipper disc

The chipper disc is standard on only a few models and is an optional extra on some but not all. It operates like the other discs but tends to produce Continental size chips, not the fat ones favoured by home-made chip connoisseurs. A useful addition if the family are great chip eaters.

Whisk

In the past the greatest criticism of food processors was their inability to whisk egg whites and whip cream. In fact it *is* possible to whip cream using the steel blade, but some manufacturers have brought out attachments to whip cream and/or whisk egg whites.

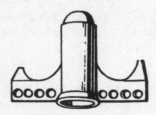

Fig. 17. A whisk.

In one case this is a plastic paddle with holes to incorporate air into the egg whites. In another case a fluted disk is fitted to the drive spindle and produces good results. A couple of models have an attachment with two traditional beaters which fit into a gearing head which in turn sits on the drive spindle. As the gearing head rotates around the bowl, the two beaters whisk the contents until egg whites are light and frothy or cream is whipped.

One food processor has a second bowl which fits within the first. It incorporates a single head rotating whisk which revolves around the bowl to whisk egg whites and whip cream. Once prepared, the second bowl can be removed and put aside, or stored in the fridge until needed.

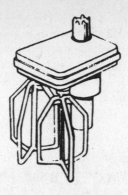

Fig. 18. A whisk with traditional beaters.

Dough kit
One manufacturer provides an extra bowl with a special domed lid to allow you to leave your mixed bread to rise in the same bowl. This frees your normal bowl and lid for other processing in the meantime.

Citrus press
If you have access to lots of citrus fruit to make fruit drinks, this is a useful attachment, otherwise a manual press is more than adequate for the small number you need to press in everyday cookery.

Juice extractor
This attachment enables you to obtain the juice of fruit and vegetables. A drum and strainer basket fit into the standard bowl but have a special cover and pusher.

19

Using Your Food Processor

All food processors operate slightly differently, so always read your handbook before first use. They are all designed to provide maximum safety and many of them won't operate if not correctly assembled. The bowl fits onto the base and is rotated to lock into position. You then fit the steel blade or other attachment. Fitting the lid correctly ensures that the machine will operate; a major safety precaution to prevent fingers reaching the sharp blades while they are still moving. With most models the lid is rotated so that lugs on the lid and bowl lock together. At the same time a projecting lug passes through a slot into the motor base, and it is this which allows the machine to run. In some of the earlier models this was the only way to switch on the processor and the lid has to be rotated smartly to and fro to produce the pulsing action. With recent models this slot in the motor base is still a safety device but there is usually an on/off switch and/or a speed and pulse control.

Keep the pusher in the feed tube during processing. It is safer to do so and it prevents food flying up at you. For the same reason, never remove the lid until the blades or disc have completely stopped.

If your machine has variable speeds, use the slower one to mince meat, chop onions and herbs, the middle speed for making cakes and yeasted mixtures, the fastest for puréeing, fine chopping, slicing and shredding.

Advice on specific areas of cooking is given in the following recipes but here are some general guidelines which may be useful:

❖ Fit the blade or whisk before adding the food.

❖ Food to be chopped should be cut evenly or the smaller pieces will be over-processed before larger ones are chopped.

❖ Don't overfill the processor bowl. For one thing liquid will spill out of the lid or onto the drive spindle, for another, solid foods will be processed unevenly. Each bowl has its recommended maximum capacity for liquids, chopping and flour mixtures, so please check your handbook.

❖ Scrape down the food. As food is processed it is flung outwards by the centrifugal force. To ensure a complete blend of ingredients, remove the lid and scrape the food from the sides to the middle, using the spatula provided.

❖ Check liquid quantity. Food processing is so efficient that you may require slightly less liquid. Add it gradually through the feed tube and check progress.

❖ Don't over-process. The blades rotate so fast it is easy to process food too long. It is far better to under-process, check and process for a further few seconds, especially when you are learning how to use your machine.

❖ Remove the bowl before the food. Twist the bowl and remove it from the motor base before removing the disc or blade, and then the food. This prevents food trickling down the drive spindle.

❖ Wash the bowl only when necessary. If ingredients are being processed separately but for use in the same recipe, it is generally unnecessary to wash the bowl and blade between operations.

20

Cooking Techniques with Food Processors

SOUPS

A soup can be a delicate starter to a dinner party, a light lunch-time snack, or a hearty meal in itself; whichever, your food processor can help you concoct creamed soups of velvety smoothness and speed up the preparation of chunky vegetable soups.

Creamed soups

If a soup is to be blended after cooking, it makes sense to cut down on cooking time by chopping the vegetables small to begin with. If a number of vegetables are to be cooked together they may also be processed together, but take care not to overload the bowl.

Onions flavour most soups, so place the peeled and quartered onion(s) into the bowl fitted with the steel blade and process until finely chopped. Additional flavourings may be added through the feed tube, dropping them in chunks onto the turning blade.

For larger quantities of the same vegetable – e.g. carrot, cauliflower, beetroot or parsnip – use the grating or slicing disc.

When puréeing a soup it is important not to overload the bowl with liquid otherwise it will leak through the spindle or lid. One solution is to halve the cooking liquid and top it up before final re-heating, or you could strain the liquid into a clean pan and spoon the solids from the sieve into the processor bowl. Take care to remove any bouquet garni or bay leaf first. Process until smooth, then transfer the purée into the liquid, scraping the sides of the bowl to capture every drop of flavouring. Stir while reheating and add milk, cream or yoghurt at this stage. Do not boil the soup after adding these unless it contains cornflour.

Chunky soups
The food processor is a great help in the preparation of soups even when they are not puréed after cooking.

The vegetables should be cut into pieces that will sit easily on a soup spoon. For example, carrots are better chopped than sliced, except when used in main course soups. Celery looks more attractive sliced rather than chopped, but the broader outer sticks should be halved lengthways to produce neater slices. When adding cabbage to a soup use the slicing disc, pressing down lightly on the pusher to ensure finely shredded strips.

PATÉS, TERRINES AND SPREADS
Use the power and speed of the steel blade to reduce cooked and uncooked meat, fish and poultry to a delightful range of pâtés, terrines and spreads. Take care not to over-process. Some pâtés are intended to be coarse in texture so process in short bursts and frequently check the appearance of the chopped ingredients.

Anyone who has to make sandwiches regularly knows how difficult it is to find something a bit different from the usual cheese, egg or cold meat filling. By using the food processor these same basic, inexpensive ingredients can be transformed into exciting spreads for more satisfying lunch-time snacks.

The same spreads provide excellent fillings for toasted sandwiches, whether made under the grill or in an electric sandwich toaster. For more interesting tea-time or supper snacks, spread the mixtures thickly on halved scones or on individual circles of shortbread.

SAUCES AND DIPS

Sauces

Sauces are intended to complement a meal, whether as an accompaniment to meat, fish, salads or puddings. The speed and simplicity of the food processor removes the mystique of sauce making, from the basic white sauce to the delicately flavoured mayonnaise and hollandaise sauces.

Certainly in the case of the quick white sauce you remove any risk of lumps and reduce the time spent standing watchfully over the stove. And homemade mayonnaise is a doddle with a food processor!

Dips

Whether served as a refreshing appetiser with crudités, or as an easy-to-eat nibble at a party, a dip is easily prepared and can be as exotic or as simple as you like.

The basis of most dips is cream cheese, mayonnaise, yoghurt or puréed vegetable, depending on the richness or sharpness of your taste. To these can be added a variety of flavourings including drained canned fish, cheeses, nuts, salad vegetables such as spring onion or green pepper, drained, canned or fresh fruit, even packet soups. The flavourings are best finely chopped or puréed using the steel blade, before adding the basis of the dip and processing until well blended.

Crudités (crisp, uncooked vegetables such as cucumber, courgette, green and red pepper, cauliflower and carrot) can be served as a starter: cut the vegetables into strips 7cm (3 in) long and about 2cm (½ in) thick. Arrange them attractively on a serving dish with a choice of two or three dips, preferably of contrasting colours, served in ramekin dishes or small pots. For a party dip, provide potato crisps, cheese sticks or Italian bread sticks.

MEAT, POULTRY, GAME AND FISH

Use your food processor to chop raw or cooked meat, blend a marinade or mix a stuffing; and if you are trying to avoid calorie-laden sauces thickened with flour, use it to purée the vegetables cooked with the meat, to form a deliciously light sauce.

140

Lovers of Chinese stir-fry can take meat straight from the freezer, cut it into pieces to fit the feed tube, and use the slicing disc to produce slivers of beef, pork or chicken (boned) that cook in seconds in a wok. Remember to remove all fat, sinews and bone before slicing.

That is the same advice when mincing uncooked meat; otherwise the fat and sinews end up wrapped around the drive shaft. When mincing uncooked, thawed meat, cut it into 3cm (1½ in) cubes and process a maximum of 340g (12 oz) at any one time. The longer the motor runs, the finer the texture of the minced (or chopped) meat, so take care not to over-process.

VEGETABLES AND SALAD

Vegetables can be prepared in seconds using the steel blade, shredding disc or slicing disc to achieve different textures. The ways of processing the most common vegetables are listed below and alternatives are included, as it is generally more convenient to process different types of vegetable into the bowl in one batch without having to change attachments.

Steel blade

When using the steel blade for chopping, only put vegetables of similar texture into the bowl together, otherwise the more fragile ones, such as mushrooms, will be puréed before the celery or pepper is finely chopped. To avoid uneven chopping, it is advisable to cut the vegetables into chunks roughly 2.5cm (1 in) square. As always, take care not to over-process raw vegetables, and use a pulsing action which allows you to check progress before everything is mashed to a pulp. When purée-ing cooked vegetables, it may be necessary to scrape smaller quantities from the sides halfway through processing to ensure a smooth texture.

Slicing disc

When using the slicing disc you may need to trim vegetables or halve them lengthways to fit the feed tube. REMEMBER NEVER TO PUSH THE FOOD DOWN THE TUBE WITH YOUR FINGERS: ALWAYS USE THE PLASTIC PUSHER. The thickness of the slices is governed by how hard you press down – the lighter the pressure, the thinner the slice.

Shredding/Grating disc

Most shredding/grating discs provided with food processors shred vegetables quite finely, although some models provide a coarser disc which produces juliennes (thin sticks) of vegetables such as carrot and other root vegetables. Use the shredding disc to mash boiled potatoes as the steel blade simply reduces them to a glutinous goo. Again, trim vegetables to fit the feed tube. If you press too firmly, very hard vegetables may form grooves and slow down the grating. Relieve the pressure a little and allow the chunks of vegetable to tumble slightly in the tube.

GUIDE TO PROCESSING VEGETABLES		
Type of Vegetable	**Method**	**Comments**
Aubergines, raw	Slice	Halve lengthways to fit the tube.
Beetroot		
– cooked	Slice or shred	For salads.
– raw	Shred	For soups or casseroles.
Cabbage		
– raw	Slice	By cutting into lengths to stand upright in feed tube, packing in tight to keep in place.
	Shred	By cutting into lengths which will lie crossways in the feed tube. Stack three-quarters up the tube and process.
	Chop	Cutting into chunks.
Celery – raw	Slice	As for carrots.
	Chop	Cut into 2.5cm/1 in lengths.
Courgettes – raw	Slice	Cut in half lengthways to fit the tube if necessary.
	Shred	For salads or stir frying.

GUIDE TO PROCESSING VEGETABLES

Type of Vegetable	Method	Comments
Cucumber	Slice	Choose a small one or halve a large one lengthways. Peel if wished.
Fennel – raw	Slice	Trim to fit tube.
	Chop	Cut into chunks.
Garlic	Chop	Preferably do at the same time as another vegetable.
Leeks – raw	Slice	Cutting to length as for carrots.
	Chop	Cutting into chunks.
Mushrooms – raw	Slice	Pack in feed tube with caps facing the sides.
	Chop	Separate stalks and pulse for 1 second at a time.
Onions – raw	Slice	Halve to fit tube.
	Grate	Halve to fit tube.
	Chop	Quarter medium/large onions.
Parsnips	Slice	As for carrots.
Peppers	Slice	Halve lengthways and deseed.
	Chop	Quarter, deseed and halve again.
Potatoes – cooked	Mash	Shred half quantity of hot potatoes, add butter and seasoning then shred remainder on top. Remove disc, stir with fork and serve.
	Slice	New potatoes when cold.

GUIDE TO PROCESSING VEGETABLES

Type of Vegetable	Method	Comments
Potatoes – raw	Slice	Trim to fit feed tube.
	Grate	Trim as above.
	Chip	If special disc provided, trimming as above.
Radishes	Slice	Pack upright in feed tube.
Swede – raw	Slice	As for potatoes.
Tomatoes – raw	Slice	Firm small tomatoes, positioning upright in feed tube.
Turnip – raw	Slice	As for potatoes.

DESSERTS

In moments fruit can be whizzed into a purée to flavour ice-cream, sorbets, mousses and fools. What quicker pudding than a drained tin of peaches puréed with a carton of cream?

Purée

When using fruit with seeds – such as raspberries, gooseberries or blackcurrants – it is worth taking the trouble to sieve the puréed fruit to remove the seeds.

Ice-creams

If your food processor doesn't have a special ice-cream making attachment, you can still use it to break down the ice crystals in the semi-frozen mixture. After processing to remove the grainy texture, the mixture will freeze down a second time to make a velvety smooth ice-cream.

PASTRIES

Anyone who has trouble making pastry, take heart: it is something a food processor does very well! The secret, of course, is the speed of preparation plus the short handling time which prevents the pastry becoming hard and tough.

If a recipe recommends a quantity of pastry, e.g. 200g/8 oz, bear in mind that this refers to the quantity of flour used, and not the total weight of the pastry. Fat is best used straight from the refrigerator and cut into 2.5cm/1 in cubes.

The table below is a guide to the ideal quantities required for different sizes of dish, plate or flan ring. Remember to adjust the fat and liquid quantities proportionately. When making batches for the freezer you should mark on each packet the flour weight for future reference. The quantity you can process in one batch is governed by the capacity of your bowl, so be guided by the manufacturer's instructions.

Because of the efficiency of blending, you may need less liquid to bind the dry ingredients of a shortcrust pastry, so add this gradually. Shortcrust pastries benefit from 30 minutes "resting" in the refrigerator before use.

GUIDE FOR MAKING PASTRY		
Dish	**Pastry Quantity**	**Size**
Shortcrust pastry Oval pie dish	150g (6 oz) covers	750ml (1½ pint) dish
	200g (8 oz) covers	1 litre (2 pint) dish
Pie plate	125g (5 oz) lines OR covers	18cm (7 in) plate
	150g (6 oz) lines OR covers	22cm (9 in) plate
	200g (8 oz) lines AND covers	18cm (7 in) plate
	250g (10 oz) lines AND covers	22cm (9 in) plate
Tartlets	200g (8 oz) makes	18 of 6cm (2½ in) diameter
		12 of 8cm (3 in) diameter

GUIDE FOR MAKING PASTRY		
Dish	**Pastry Quantity**	**Size**
Flan ring	125g (5 oz) lines	18cm (7 in) ring
	150g (6 oz) lines	20cm (8 in) ring
Puff Pastry		
Oval pie dish	100g (4 oz) covers	1 litre (2 pint) dish
Suet Pastry		
Pudding basin	200g (8 oz) lines AND covers	750ml (1½ pint) basin
	300g (12 oz) lines AND covers	1.4 litre (2½ pint) basin
Dumplings	200g (8 oz) makes	16 of medium size

Flan cases

Apart from pastry you can use some more unusual linings for your flans, sweet and savoury – such as biscuit crumb or oatflake cases – and the food processor will help with the initial chopping of ingredients, as well as the blending.

BREAD

Anyone who has been overawed by the complications of bread-making can now bake the most delicious rolls, loaves and yeasted breads. A food processor can only manage a relatively small amount of dough in one batch, compared with the traditional kneading method; however, for many people it is still quicker to make up three batches in the processor. Most manufacturers recommend a maximum mixture using 450g/1 lb flour, and some manufacturers recommend resting the processor for an hour or two after five consecutive operations.

Yeast can be bought in two forms: either as compressed fresh yeast from health food shops, some chemists and bakers or dried yeast. Fresh yeast will keep for up to 2 weeks in the refrigerator in a small plastic box, or loosely wrapped in a polythene bag. It may also be frozen for up to 6 weeks, divided into usable portions and well wrapped. Blend the frozen yeast straight into the warm liquid or thaw for 20 minutes before use.

Dried yeast keeps for up to a year while sealed. Once opened store in a *small* airtight container and use within 4 months; so buy in small amounts to ensure freshness.

Blend fresh yeast with hand-hot liquid (38°C/100°F). Don't cream the yeast with the sugar or the bread will taste unpleasantly yeasty. Dried yeast is reconstituted by stirring it with a little sugar into hand-hot liquid, leaving it for 10 minutes in a warm place until the yeast has dissolved and the mixture froths. If there is no froth, the yeast is stale and should not be used.

Bread can be made with white, wheatmeal or wholewheat (granary) flour. Best results are obtained with strong flours which are high in gluten-forming proteins.

Rising time will vary depending on the temperature of the room:

1 hour in a warm room not above 32°C (90°F)
1½ hours at room temperature 18-21°C (65-70°F)
4 hours in a cool place.

CAKES, SCONES AND BISCUITS

Cake making with a food processor is faster and less strenuous than the arm-aching wooden spoon method; but do not expect the same lighter-than-air sponges which can only be created by beating in air either by hand or using a food mixer. Most food processors cannot incorporate the same amount of air and instead the all-in-one method (e.g. Victoria Sandwich) uses baking powder as well as self-raising flour to achieve the extra rise.

If you have a food processor capable of whisking egg whites, you will be able to produce the traditional type of sponges by following the manufacturer's instructions. When converting your own recipes, take care when adding the liquid as you may require slightly less when using your food processor.

When mixing, do so in short bursts, periodically scraping down mixture from the sides. Always add dried fruit, glacé cherries and chocolate chips last of all, using a pulsing action, otherwise the steel blade will chop them out of recognition.

Use your food processor to make marzipan and icing to decorate the cakes.

MISCELLANEOUS

❖ Biscuit crumbs: halve the biscuits, such as digestives, and drop through the feed tube on the turning blades.

❖ Breadcrumbs: use any type of bread, sliced or unsliced, with crusts removed. Break sliced bread into quarters and tear unsliced bread into 2.5cm (1 in) cubes. Fill the bowl no more than half full then process for a few seconds until the breadcrumbs are formed. Store in plastic bags and freeze until required. Keep white and brown breadcrumbs separate for different uses.

❖ Butters: delicious as an accompaniment to grilled steaks or spread between thick slices of French stick and reheated in the oven. For herb butter process 100g (4 oz) butter with 2 tbsp dried mixed herbs; for garlic butter process two peeled garlic cloves until finely chopped, add 100g (4 oz) butter and process until well blended; for anchovy butter, drain the fillets from a 50g (2 oz) can of anchovies and process with 100g (4 oz) butter and 1 tsp lemon juice. If to be used with steaks, prepare the butter several hours in advance, shape into a roll, wrap in foil and refrigerate for an hour at least. Cut into slices and place on top of the meat just before serving.

❖ Cheese: if grating, hard cheese should be cut into 2.5cm (1½ in) cubes and processed using the steel blade for 20-30 seconds until finely chopped. Softer (not cream) cheese should be grated using the grating disc. Quantities of grated cheese may be bagged and sealed and kept for a few days in the refrigerator or frozen. Use straight from the freezer for sauces and general cooking. If slicing, use the slicing disc with firm cheese and trim the cheese to fit the feed tube.

❖ Chocolate: chill the chocolate then break into small, even chunks. Put into the cold bowl and process with the steel blade until finely chopped.

❖ Cream making: keep unsalted butter in the refrigerator and you have the basis of stand-by cream at any time, and at half the price. It is slightly heavier than fresh

148

cream but the addition of chopped zest of lemon or other fruit will mask this fact. Chill the cream well before whipping and take care not to over-whip – it is best to use a hand whisk. Use soon after whipping and use any of these creams within 2 days of making. When flavouring with chocolate, use grated chocolate rather than melted chocolate which causes this home-made cream to curdle. It will not freeze.

GUIDE TO CREAM MAKING		
Type of Cream	Unsalted Butter	Milk
Pouring cream	75g (3 oz)	100ml (4 fl oz)
Whipping cream	100g (4 oz)	100ml (4 fl oz)
Double cream	125g (5 oz)	100ml (4 fl oz)

Cut the butter into small pieces about 1cm/½ in cube and heat with the milk until melted. Do not boil. Pour into the bowl and process with three 10-second pulses. Pour into a bowl or jug and refrigerate for at least 2 hours, preferably overnight for whipping cream.

❖ Crisps: use the slicing disc to slice potatoes very thinly. Wash well in cold water, drain on a cloth and pat dry. Deep fry in hot fat, a small quantity at a time. When golden brown remove, drain on kitchen paper, season with salt and serve warm or cold.

❖ Dried fruits: to chop dried fruits such as apricots, prunes (stoned), glacé cherries, dates, etc., first chill them for about 1 hour. Process with a little of the flour taken from the recipe.

21

Care of Your Food Processor

Always switch off and disconnect the appliance before cleaning. Clean the plastic casing of the motor base with a damp, not wet, cloth. The plastic bowl and lid should be washed in hot, soapy water, rinsed and dried. Check the manufacturer's handbook as to whether they may be washed in a dishwasher.

The blades and discs should be washed similarly but ensure that there is no food lodged in the grating holes. It may be necessary to use a bottle brush to clean up inside the stem of the blade; some models are poorly designed and have awkward food traps. A dishwasher can be ideal to get them really clean.

When not in use, secure the bowl and steel blade and fit the lid loosely with the pusher in position. This allows a slight airflow to prevent mustiness over a long period. Don't leave the lid locked into the motor base.

22

Recipes

WHITE SAUCE

FOR COATING:
25g/1 oz softened butter
25g/1 oz cornflour
250ml/½ pint milk

FOR POURING:
15g/½ oz softened butter
15g/½ oz cornflour
250ml/½ pint milk

The method for both types of sauce is the same:

1.   Put the ingredients into the bowl and process until well blended, then transfer to a heavy based milkpan, preferably non-stick.

2.   Bring to the boil, stirring continuously and cook for a further 2 minutes. (Always use a medium heat with a white sauce as a fierce heat could burn the bottom of the sauce.)

3.   If you do make a lumpy sauce, return it to the bowl for a quick whizz until smooth.

MAYONNAISE

1 egg, size 3 *(and a second yolk for a thicker mayonnaise)*
salt and pepper
¼ tsp dry mustard
2 tbsp wine vinegar
300ml/½ pint olive oil

1. Have all the ingredients at room temperature.

2. Put the egg, seasoning and vinegar into the bowl and process briefly until well blended.

3. Remove the plastic pusher and, with the motor still running, pour the oil through the filling tube in a thin, steady stream.

4. If the mayonnaise should curdle during this stage, add a few more drops of vinegar and process before adding more oil. If this mixture is still curdled, pour it into a jug, wash and dry the bowl and steel blade, and start again with another egg yolk, gradually adding the curdled mixture and then the remaining oil.

5. At this stage adjust the seasoning or add other flavourings if desired.

CREAM OF CAULIFLOWER SOUP

Serves 4-6

1 head of cauliflower, separated into florets
550ml/1 pint vegetable stock
15ml/1 tbsp cornflour
300ml/½ pint milk
salt and pepper
croûtons to garnish

1.   Use the slicing disc to slice the cauliflower florets. Put the sliced cauliflower into a large saucepan and add the stock. Cook until softened.

2.   Fit the steel blade. Strain the cooking liquid into a clean pan and process the cauliflower until puréed.

3.   Add the cornflour and milk and process until well blended.

4.   Stir into the liquid and bring to the boil over a medium heat, stirring continuously.

5.   Simmer for a few minutes, season and serve sprinkled with hot croûtons.

CHICKEN LIVER PÂTÉ

Serves 6-8

1 onion, quartered
clove garlic (*optional*)
25g/1 oz butter
450g/1 lb chicken livers
salt and freshly ground black pepper
1 egg
2 tbsp sherry

1. Process the onion and garlic until finely chopped.

2. Melt the butter in a frypan and fry the onion and garlic gently until softened but not browned.

3. Remove any skin or gall from the livers and add the livers to the frypan. Fry briefly until browned on all sides, then transfer to the bowl and add all the remaining ingredients. Process until smoothly blended.

4. Pour into a greased 500ml/1 pint soufflé dish and cover with foil. Stand in a baking tin and pour into the tin sufficient boiling water to come half-way up the dish. Cook in the middle of the oven (170°C/325°F/Gas Mark 3) for about 1 hour.

5. Remove from the oven and place a weight over the pâté to compress it. Serve when cold.

VEGETARIAN SUPPER LOAF

Serves 6

225g/8 oz mature Cheddar cheese
bunch of fresh parsley
50g/2 oz rye crispbread, broken into pieces
1 green pepper, de-seeded and quartered
1 onion, peeled and quartered
25g/1 oz butter
8 eggs
198g/7 oz can of sweetcorn and mixed peppers
salt and black pepper

1. Cut the cheese into chunks and process until finely chopped. Remove from the bowl.

2. Process the parsley with the crispbread until finely chopped. Remove from the bowl.

3. Process the green pepper and onion until finely chopped and fry in the butter until softened.

4. Process the eggs in the bowl until well blended and add the cheese, parsley, crispbread, pepper and onion and all the remaining ingredients. Process with short pulses to ensure mixture is well blended.

5. Grease a large loaf tin and line the base with greased greaseproof paper. Pour the mixture into the tin and bake at 180°C/350°F/Gas Mark 4 for 1-1¼ hours or until just set. Allow to cool then turn out.

6. Serve with salad.

POTATO AND MUSHROOM PIE

Serves 4

fresh parsley
3 cloves garlic
100g/4 oz butter
salt and black pepper
1kg/2 lb potatoes
100g/4 oz button mushrooms
milk

1. Process the parsley to produce about 2 tablespoonfuls of chopped parsley. Add the garlic and process until crushed.

2. Add the butter and ½ tsp of salt and process until well blended. Scrape from the bowl and keep to one side.

3. Fit the slicing disc and slice the potatoes very thinly, remove then slice the wiped mushrooms.

4. Rub the base and sides of a wide diameter, fairly shallow dish, with a little of the garlic butter. Layer half the mushrooms into the dish and top with half the potato. Season with black pepper and repeat with the remaining mushrooms and finally arrange a neat lid of potato slices. Sprinkle with black pepper.

5. Melt the garlic butter and pour over the potatoes. Top up with milk, leaving a margin for the liquid to boil up during cooking, otherwise it will boil over.

6. Cover with greased aluminium foil and bake for 1½ hours at 170°C/325°F/Gas Mark 3. Remove the foil, boost the heat to 200°C/400°F/Gas Mark 6 and brown for a further half hour.

SPICY CASSEROLE OF LAMB

Serves 4

50g/2 oz dried apricots
1 large onion, peeled and quartered
397g/14 oz can of tomatoes
1 tbsp peanut butter
salt and pepper
700g/1½ lb lean stewing lamb, cubed
1 tbsp oil
700g/1½ lb potatoes, peeled

1. Process the halved apricots until finely chopped.

2. Add the onion and chop coarsely.

3. Add the tomatoes, peanut butter and seasoning and process to blend.

4. Brown the meat in the oil in a flameproof casserole. Pour the sauce over.

5. Fit the slicing disc, slice the potatoes, and arrange as a lid over the meat.

6. Cook for 1½ hours in a medium oven, 190°C/375°F/ Gas Mark 5.

SWEET AND SOUR CHICKEN

Serves 4

1 onion, peeled and quartered
1 green pepper, de-seeded and quartered
1 stick of celery, cut into 4
4 chicken joints
1 tbsp oil
227g/8 oz can of pineapple slices or chunks
1 tbsp cornflour
4 tbsp wine vinegar
1 tbsp soy sauce
50g/2 oz brown sugar
salt and pepper

1. Put the onion, green pepper and celery into the bowl and process until coarsely chopped.

2. Brown the chicken joints in the oil in a large lidded frypan. Remove the chicken from the pan and keep on one side. Gently fry the vegetables in the remaining oil until softened but not browned.

3. Drain the pineapple juice from the can into a measuring jug and add sufficient water to make 300ml/½ pint. Put this liquid into the bowl with the pineapple and all the remaining ingredients. Add the fried vegetables.

4. Process until the sauce is well blended.

5. Return the chicken to the frypan, pour over the sauce, cover and bring to the boil. Reduce the heat to simmering and cook for 15-25 minutes, depending on the thickness of the chicken.

STRAWBERRY CREAM MOUSSE

Serves 4-6

6 tbsp water
1 sachet gelatine
450g/1 lb strawberries
225g/8 oz curd cheese
2 eggs, separated
50g/2 oz caster sugar
150ml/¼ pint double cream

1. Put the water into a cup and sprinkle on the gelatine. Stand the cup in a pan of hot water until the gelatine is dissolved.

2. Wipe and hull the strawberries, reserving a few for decoration. Put into a bowl and purée. Add the cheese and process until well blended.

3. Add the egg yolks, sugar, cream and dissolved gelatine and blend well together.

4. Whisk the egg whites until they form stiff peaks, and with one short burst incorporate them into the strawberry mixture.

5. Pour into a mould and leave to set in the refrigerator.

6. To unmould, dip for a few seconds in hot water and turn out onto a serving dish. Decorate with whipped cream and fresh strawberries.

GINGERBREAD

100g/4 oz margarine
150g/6 oz black treacle
50g/2 oz golden syrup
125ml/¼ pint milk
200g/8 oz plain flour
1 tbsp ground ginger
1 tsp bicarbonate of soda
1 tsp mixed spice
50g/2 oz caster sugar
2 eggs, beaten
50g/2 oz sultanas

1. Grease and line a large loaf tin.

2. Put the margarine, treacle and golden syrup into a medium saucepan and warm together, but don't allow to boil. Remove from the heat, stir in the milk and allow to cool.

3. Put the flour, ginger, bicarbonate of soda, mixed spice and sugar into the bowl and pulse to blend.

4. Add the cooled liquid and eggs, and process until completely blended. Add the sultanas and pulse to mix.

5. Turn into the loaf tin and bake at 150°C, 300°F, Gas Mark 2 for 1¼ hours. Cool in the tin for 10 minutes before turning out onto a cooling rack.

Slow Cooking

23

Slow Cookers

Since electric slow cookers first arrived in this country, many years ago, people have come to recognise the advantages of this means of cooking. Once slow cooking was a way of life – food would be prepared in the morning and left to cook all day in the range beside the kitchen fire. By the time the family returned home in the evening a delicious meal would be ready and waiting. Most modern kitchens don't have room for a cooking range but the advantages of slow cooking are still appreciated.

A slow cooker is an electrical appliance designed to cook gently and safely, unattended, for many hours. Food won't burn, boil or dry up in a slow cooker because it cooks at such gentle temperatures. Most slow cookers have two cooking settings: LOW, to cook all day or overnight, and HIGH to cook for mid-day or for shorter periods.

A slow cooker makes delicious soups, stews and casseroles, but isn't limited only to this type of cooking. With its gentle cooking, fish and delicate fruit and vegetables remain whole, even after long cooking. Joints of meat 'roasted' in a slow cooker retain their juices and shrinkage is reduced. By using the slow cooker as a water bath or bain marie you can prepare delightfully smooth pâté and light-textured sponges and suet puddings. Even mulled wine or warming hot punches can be prepared and served in a slow cooker to make a success of any party.

Why cook slowly?

Food which has been cooked slowly tastes so much better because the flavours have had time to develop and blend. Cooking meat over a long period at a gentle heat in moist conditions breaks down the tissue and the meat becomes tender. Slow cooking will tenderise even the tougher cuts of meat such as shin of beef, oxtail and neck of lamb, and the resulting dish will be deliciously succulent.

Unlike microwave or pressure cooking, slow cooking is relatively imprecise and this is one of its greatest advantages as it allows flexible meal times. For example, after six hours a casserole may be cooked but after ten hours it is still just as good. Even two hours later it is perhaps past its best but still very acceptable. No more frayed nerves when family or guests arrive late for a meal!

Very little steam escapes during slow cooking and this has a number of benefits:

❖ The flavour of food is retained.

❖ Smells don't escape into the kitchen.

❖ The kitchen is kept free of steam and the walls and windows don't run with condensation.

❖ Steamed puddings don't dry up and need topping up with water.

A slow cooker can help reduce housekeeping bills too. Tasty, nourishing meals can be provided using cheaper cuts of meat which demand long, slow cooking to make them tender. Electricity can be saved by using a slow cooker instead of an oven. An electric oven has to heat a bigger space, even to cook one casserole, and therefore consumes more power. A slow cooker is more economical because it operates at a low wattage, often using no more current than a light bulb. The light left on all night to comfort a nervous child uses the same amount of electricity as the slow cooker does to cook a meal. Savings vary from model to model and depend on what is being cooked: a stew cooked in a slow cooker consuming 75

164

watts uses 50 per cent less electricity than in a conventional oven; with a crème caramel the saving is as high as 80 per cent.

A slow cooker heats the food inside it and not the whole kitchen, as is the case with a conventional oven. Even during the summer we need to cook and a slow cooker can prepare food which is to be eaten cold later. Pâté, soup for chilling, roast chicken, ham, crème caramel and pears in red wine can all be left to cook without an oven heating the kitchen to heatwave temperatures.

Slow cookers are absolutely safe to leave cooking unattended all day or all night, just as you would leave the refrigerator or freezer running while you are out. As an added guarantee of safety, slow cookers have to be approved to meet European safety standards.

Who uses a slow cooker?

Ask people why they use a slow cooker and you will be given a number of different answers, depending upon their way of life.

❖ *Students* in rented accommodation may have limited facilities, perhaps only a single cooking ring. With a slow cooker they can eat a balanced diet, economically, at flexible times and without neighbours complaining about cooking smells.

❖ *People out at work* can return home weary at the end of the day to a tasty hot meal.

❖ *Parents with young or school-age children* can prepare a family meal in advance. If the family can't all sit down together for the meal, that's no problem: those who need to eat earlier have theirs and the remaining portions continue cooking on LOW until the others sit down to eat an hour or two later. After-school activities, travel hold-ups, shift work – no problem! Meals can be flexible and the food isn't spoilt for the latecomer.

❖ *Elderly people*, often on limited incomes. Economic savings in food bills and heating costs have already been described.

24

How to Choose a Slow Cooker

There are so many different electric slow cookers on the market that the choice is often difficult. The following will explain the differences.

Lid

The lid is usually made of stoneware. As stoneware is subject to greater variations of manufacture than is the case with pressed glass or moulded plastic, you may find that the lids vary in colour and may have slight marks in the glaze. This is one of the characteristics of stoneware and doesn't indicate inferior quality. The lid should fit loosely onto the pot and may be slid from side to side. It should not rock, however, as that could allow precious heat to escape. During cooking, condensation gathers around the lid of the pot forming an important water seal with the lid. If the lid rocks, the seal may not form.

Pot

Slow cookers contain a cooking pot usually made of stoneware, an excellent insulator of heat. The capacity of the pots varies from 1.5 litres (2½ pints) to 3.1 litres (5.4 pints). Some pots are narrow and deep and others are wide and shallow, depending on the location of the heat source. Pudding basins fit more easily into a deep pot but a shallow pot is better when

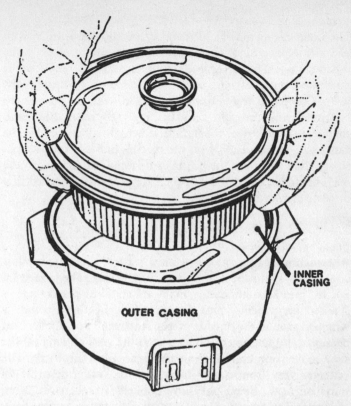

INNER CASING

OUTER CASING

Fig. 19. Typical slow cooker with removable stoneware pot.

cooking food like stuffed peppers or trout. The larger the
base, the more peppers or trout can be cooked at one time.

All slow cookers can be filled to within 15mm/½ in of the
brim, without danger of boiling over. Models with a capacity
of about 2.5 litres/4.4 pints are large enough for a family of
four but are also suitable for only one or two people. Even a
1½kg/3 lb chicken can be cooked whole in this size. If you
cook for four or more, own a freezer or entertain frequently, a
capacity of about 3.1 litres/5.4 pints would be ideal.

There are two types of slow cooker: those with a fixed pot
and those with a removable pot.

Removable pot slow cookers

The outer casing may be of metal or plastic and is fitted with an inner metal casing. The removable stoneware pot sits in the inner casing. The heating element is situated between the inner and outer casings, either on the base or around the walls. Compared with a fixed pot slow cooker, the heat has to be transferred through an extra layer to reach the food, therefore the electrical consumption is higher; between 80-105 watts on LOW, depending on the model. But it is still cheaper to use than an oven. The pot may be removed and put in the oven or under the grill for special toppings and washed in a bowl or dishwasher.

Fixed pot slow cookers

Although no longer sold, you may 'inherit' this type of slow cooker, the first model to appear in the UK. The stoneware pot fits into an outer casing made of metal or plastic, and is screwed permanently into position. The heating element is wrapped around the outside of the stoneware pot. As the heat passes from the element directly into the wall of the pot, the slow cooker only consumes a small amount of electricity. The wattages vary from model to model and range from 55-75 watts on LOW. Fixed pot slow cookers are therefore more economical to run. As the electrical fittings are permanently attached they must not be immersed in water when washing.

Heat settings

Generally slow cookers have two cooking settings: LOW and HIGH. LOW is used for all day or all night cooking and HIGH is used to speed up cooking, say for midday, and can reduce the cooking time to just over half that for LOW. HIGH is also used to cook certain foods requiring faster penetration of heat, such as joints of meat, whole poultry, pâté and steamed puddings.

It is impossible to relate LOW and HIGH to the settings of gas or electric ovens. If manufacturers' instructions are followed, the temperature of the cooking liquid will reach just below 100°C (boiling point) which is hot enough to cook the food thoroughly and safely. This temperature is achieved on both settings but is reached more quickly on HIGH, in this way accelerating cooking.

At the beginning of cooking it is important to raise the temperature as quickly as possible to destroy any harmful bacteria which may be present. This is achieved in different ways, depending on the model's construction and wattage, and it is worth reading the manufacturers' instructions before buying as it could influence your choice of slow cooker.

For example, some manufacturers recommend that you pre-heat the slow cooker on HIGH while you prepare your ingredients, as with an oven. After adding the food the slow cooker stays on HIGH for about 20 minutes before switching down to LOW: so if you leave home at 8.30 am you would need to put the food in the slow cooker by 8.10 am. One model overcomes the need to wait by incorporating an automatic setting. On AUTO the slow cooker heats up on HIGH and, by means of a thermostat, automatically switches down to LOW when the required temperature is reached. Further variations include a slow cooker which has only one setting and is only intended for all-day cooking.

Indicator lights

Some slow cookers are fitted with an indicator light to show that they are switched on in use. This is particularly useful as a slow cooker heats up slowly and, without an indicator light, it is possible to leave the house thinking that the slow cooker is switched on when, in fact, perhaps, the plug hasn't been pushed in properly. Upon return the food is cold and uncooked!

Flex and plug

A detachable electric flex means that slow cookers can be taken to the table, or cleaned more easily if the pot is fixed.

It is very important to fit a plug with a 3-amp fuse to a slow cooker rather than one with a 13-amp fuse. If something were to go wrong electrically, the 3-amp fuse would blow before the slow cooker became damaged. If it were fitted with a 13-amp fuse a greater surge of electricity would get through before it blew and this could damage the slow cooker. A higher rated fuse does *not* make the slow cooker cook more quickly.

Also, it is *not* advisable to plug a slow cooker into a time-switch. Food should not be left standing at room temperature and the heat rise from cold when the slow cooker does begin to heat may not be adequate in some slow cookers to cook food safely.

Buying for use abroad

If you intend buying a slow cooker to use abroad, first determine the local voltage in that country. All slow cookers sold in Britain are rated for 240 volts supply. In Eire, Northern Ireland and on the Continent the supply is mainly 220 volts and in America 110 volts. A 240-volt slow cooker will not work efficiently on 220 volts and hardly at all on 110 volts. Check with manufacturers because they may produce special export models with the correct wattage.

25

Using a Slow Cooker

Each type of slow cooker differs slightly and it is therefore essential to follow manufacturers' basic instructions for best results. For example, they may recommend that your slow cooker be pre-heated on HIGH *while ingredients are prepared and then kept on* HIGH *for a time before switching to* LOW. *If this is the case you should follow that basic pattern, even if not specified in the following recipes. The cooking times will be approximately the same.*

Preparation
Using a slow cooker requires a certain amount of forethought but once you have devised your own method of preparation slow cooking will become automatic. Below is a suggested pattern which you may find useful, especially if you are short of time in the morning.

1. Assemble ingredients the previous evening. If the meat is still in the freezer, remove first and prepare last, allowing it time to thaw partially at room temperature.

2. Peel any root vegetables and store covered in cold water in a sealed container in the refrigerator. Chop onion and store, covered, in the fridge.

3. Measure into a shallow bowl any flour to be used for thickening. Add required seasoning, mix and cover.

171

4. If the meat is unfrozen, trim fat and cut to the required size. If the meat is too frozen to cube, it may still be possible to trim excess fat. (This is often easier to do whilst partially frozen.) Cover the meat and store overnight in the refrigerator.

5. DO NOT STORE UNCOOKED FOOD IN THE SLOW COOKER EITHER AT ROOM TEMPERATURE OR IN THE REFRIGERATOR.

6. In the morning, if pre-heating is recommended, switch the slow cooker to HIGH as soon as you arrive in the kitchen.

7. Take ingredients from the refrigerator, boil the kettle for your morning drink and perhaps also to dissolve a stock cube. Chop the root vegetables and, if necessary, cube the meat.

There are two basic ways of preparing a savoury recipe. One is the Browning method and the other is the One-Step method.

Browning method
Browning can improve the appearance and flavour of many recipes, although some people prefer not to do this – the choice is yours. The Browning method is not used for fish, skinned chicken and some white stews containing lamb, pork or veal where the meat need not be coloured.

1. Heat a little fat or oil in a large, deep frypan. Meanwhile, switch on the slower cooker on HIGH.

2. Fry the thinly sliced or diced flavouring vegetables (i.e. onion, celery, carrot, etc.) over a medium heat. Stir occasionally until softened and starting to brown – about 5 minutes. Transfer to the slow cooker using a slotted spoon.

3. For a thickened soup or casserole, toss the pieces of meat in flour. Brown on all sides in the frypan. When

172

browning a joint, turn on all sides for even colour. Transfer the browned meat to the slow cooker, using a slotted spoon.

4.   If you have a deep frypan or use a large saucepan, it is possible to leave the vegetables and meat in the pan, then add herbs, seasoning and cooking liquid, bringing everything to the boil, stirring until the flour has thickened the sauce. Alternatively, sprinkle the herbs and seasoning over the food in the slow cooker and pour in the hot cooking liquid. Switch to LOW for all-day cooking.

One-Step method
Follow this method if you are short of time, following a low fat diet, preparing a white stew or if you simply prefer not to brown food.

1.   Switch the slow cooker to HIGH while assembling or preparing ingredients.

2.   Ensure vegetables such as onions, carrots, potatoes, celery and turnips are cut small and put into the slow cooker first.

3.   Add the meat or skinned poultry.

4.   Add herbs and seasoning and pour over sufficient hot cooking liquid barely to cover the food. Always ensure that the vegetables are immersed in the liquid. Switch to LOW and add 2-3 hours to the minimum recommended cooking time.

Cooking settings and times
After the food has been put into the slow cooker, select the setting which suits your day. Recipes usually recommend minimum and maximum cooking times for LOW but you can work out the time for HIGH – it's just over half that needed on LOW.

HIGH is used throughout cooking for certain recipes. Steamed puddings which include a raising agent need a higher temperature to ensure that the sponge or suet mixture rises. Pâtés, whole poultry and *joints* of meat should be cooked only on HIGH to ensure quick heat penetration into the solid mass to destroy any harmful bacteria which may be present.

Some foods don't cook satisfactorily if left all day. These include some fish, pasta, rice and most desserts. Nevertheless, they are ideal for lunch-time or half-day cooking.

As all slow cookers operate slightly differently, it may be necessary to adjust the times given in the recipes. As a rule of thumb, compare the times given with those in your instruction booklet. This comparison will indicate whether you should increase or reduce the cooking times.

During cooking
After fitting the lid it is best to forget about the slow cooker until you are ready to serve the food. Resist the temptation to lift the lid and peep. The water seal around the rim will be broken, releasing heat, and will take some time to form again. The food shouldn't be stirred until the end of cooking, unless recommended in the recipe. During the first hour the slow cooker is heating up to cooking temperature. If heat is lost at this stage it will add considerably to the cooking time. Approximately 20 minutes should be added to the cooking time whenever the lid is removed during the first half of cooking.

Make sure that the slow cooker stands on a heat-resistant surface during cooking as the heat from the base could harm a highly polished surface such as a dining table. Furthermore, some slow cookers may spit slightly when cooking on HIGH. This indicates a slight build-up of pressure venting through the water seal and should not cause any great inconvenience. If the slow cooker stands in a draught or cold kitchen in winter, the cooking time may need to be extended by an hour.

After cooking
The slow cooker will continue cooking until it is switched off at the plug. If some of the food is to be eaten by a latecomer within the next few hours, leave the slow cooker switched on, set at LOW. If some of the food is to be eaten another day the

extra portions should be removed from the slow cooker as soon as it is switched off. As with all methods of cooking, the food should be transferred to a clean container and cooled quickly before refrigerating or freezing. Never leave food to cool slowly in the slow cooker as stoneware retains heat, even overnight.

The temperature rise of a slow cooker is not fast enough to re-heat cooked food. This should be done in a saucepan or oven.

26

Getting the Best From Your Slow Cooker

When adapting one of your own recipes for use in a slow cooker, remember that the slowest cooking ingredients, such as carrots, potatoes and dried beans, will dictate the cooking time. If in doubt, write to the manufacturer for their advice. The following points are worth bearing in mind:

❖ *Frozen foods*: Fish, meat, poultry and game must be completely thawed before cooking. Quickly cooked frozen vegetables (i.e. peas, beans, sweetcorn) may be thawed and added during the final half hour of cooking.

❖ *Vegetables* take longer to cook in a slow cooker than meat. Place them in the hottest part of the pot (bottom or sides, depending on where the element is situated) and ensure they are completely immersed during cooking. Root and other slow cooking vegetables should be cut into thin (5mm/¼ inch) slices or diced. If possible, sauté or parboil vegetables before cooking.

❖ *Flavour:* Since there is little loss of liquid through evaporation, the juices are concentrated and most flavour is retained. Don't use too many herbs or strongly flavoured vegetables while you are getting to know your slow cooker.

❖ *Cooking liquid:* This can be water, stock, water and stock cube, wine, beer, cider, fruit juice or soup. You won't need as much liquid as in conventional cooking since there is less evaporation and also the juices from the meat and vegetables are conserved in the stock. Consequently you are usually left with more liquid than at the beginning. (Packet soups should be prepared using half the recommended amount of water to make a quick basis for a casserole.)

❖ *Milk:* Apart from when used in milk puddings, cream and milk should not be used for slow cooking as they tend to separate. If wished, milk may be added during the last half hour of cooking and cream just before serving.

❖ *Thickening:* Juices from the meat and vegetables will thin the sauce during cooking, so you should start with a thicker sauce than usual. If using the Browning method, toss the meat in flour before frying, or add flour or cornflour blended with a little cold water to the cooking liquid before boiling, stirring continuously until thickened. If using the One-Step method, turn the slow cooker to HIGH for the last 30 minutes' cooking and stir in cornflour blended with a little cold water. Always thicken with cornflour if the dish is to be frozen.

❖ *Pasta:* Only add pasta during the last 30 minutes of cooking or it becomes too soft. Lasagne should be softened before use by cooking in boiling water for 5 minutes. All pasta should be totally immersed in the sauce to ensure even cooking.

❖ *Rice:* Easy-cook long grain rice is best for savoury dishes. When rice is used as the main ingredient it should be stirred a couple of times during cooking to ensure even absorption of liquid. If a casserole or soup is to be cooked all day, add the rice 30 minutes before serving. The rice will absorb some of the liquid at the beginning. Allow an extra 150ml/¼ pint for each 50g/2 oz rice.

❖ *Dried beans:* These should be soaked overnight in plenty of water (with a teaspoonful of bicarbonate of soda to aid softening, if desired) before slow cooking. Next day, drain and rinse the beans and fast boil in the cooking liquid in a pan for 15 minutes before adding to the slow cooker. This is particularly important when cooking dried red kidney beans in a slow cooker, saucepan or in the oven, to destroy the toxin which they contain in the raw or undercooked state. Season dried beans *after* cooking as salt added before toughens the skins. Lentils don't need pre-soaking.

❖ *Toppings:* If the stoneware pot is removable you can add toppings to the cooked food and put the pot into the oven or under the grill to finish cooking. For example: piped mashed potato, grated cheese, scone topping, French bread with mustard and grated cheese on a soup or casserole, a crumble or meringue mixture over cooked fruit.

Troubleshooting

As with any new method of cooking you may need to try it a few times before you feel at home with slow cooking. Below are some of the more common problems experienced by new slow cooker users.

❖ The food was put into the slow cooker hot but was cold and uncooked at the end of the recommended cooking time. Was the plug pushed properly into the slow cooker? Could it have been knocked out during cooking?

❖ The food isn't cooked within the recommended time. If using the One-Step method have you added 2-3 hours to the minimum recommended time? Did you add hot stock if recommended in the recipe? Is the slow cooker standing in a cold draught or cold kitchen? If the lid fits badly, change it. Cooking can be speeded up by placing a circle of aluminium foil over the surface of the food.

❖ The meat is cooked but the vegetables are still crunchy. Are the vegetables cut small enough? Are they immersed in the liquid?

❖ The gravy or sauce is too thin. Use less liquid than a conventional recipe or add more thickening at the beginning or end of cooking.

❖ The food is sometimes brown and 'crusty' on top after 10 hours' cooking. Simply stir the casserole before serving and next time add a little more liquid.

❖ The potatoes have turned black and are uncooked. Are they protruding above the liquid? Ensure that they are fully immersed next time.

❖ The vegetables are cooked but the meat is still tough. If you have a particularly tough piece of meat or fowl it may need a couple of hours longer cooking than is suggested in a recipe.

❖ There is an odd smell when the slow cooker is operating. This could be caused by the new plastic insulation and fittings being heated for the first few times. If the smell persists, contact the manufacturer.

❖ You arrive home early or for one of the above reasons the meal isn't ready. Turn to HIGH to speed up the cooking.

Don't be discouraged if your first attempt isn't quite right. Even the most experienced cook has to adapt techniques slightly. Try to discover what went wrong and, if in doubt, write to the manufacturer who has experts on hand to answer such queries.

Equipment

The correct equipment makes cooking a lot easier. The following are invaluable and used when slow cooking.

For browning and sautéing, a deep non-stick frypan or saucepan made of thick aluminium allows you to fry fatty meat with little or no oil or fat.

Use a slotted or perforated spoon to transfer fried meat or vegetables to the slow cooker and the majority of fat is left in

Fig. 20. Deep non-stick frypan – ideal for pre-browning.

the pan. A set of measuring spoons ensures that you add the correct proportion of herbs, seasoning, thickening, etc.

When cooking puddings, pâtés or cakes, ensure that the container fits inside the slow cooker without raising the lid. As the lid is usually slightly domed, it is surprising how large a basin will fit. A 1 litre/2 pint basin may be too big for some smaller slow cookers but a soufflé dish of the same capacity will fit easily. If the container fits so snugly that it is difficult to lift out, make a lifting strap by taking a piece of foil 60cm x 30cm/2 ft x 1 ft and folding it in half lengthways. Fold in half again to make a strap 60cm/2 ft long and 75mm/3 in wide. Pass the strap under the container, hold both ends tightly together and lift the container into the slow cooker. Leave in position during cooking and use the strap to lift the hot pudding from the slow cooker. After use, the strap can be dried and used again and again.

A liquidiser or blender is invaluable when preparing soups.

Care of your slow cooker

❖ The stoneware pot will break if dropped, chip if knocked hard, and sudden changes in temperature could also damage it – so don't put it in the refrigerator, freezer or onto the gas or electric hob!

❖ The stoneware or glass lid is also vulnerable.

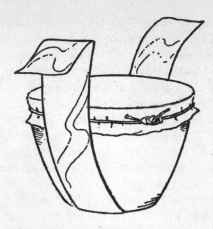

Fig. 21. Lifting strap on pudding basin.

❖ Don't pre-heat the outer casing without the cold pot being in place.

❖ Thaw frozen food before use.

❖ Use oven gloves when removing a hot stoneware pot from the slow cooker and stand on a cloth or chopping board rather than on a cold surface.

❖ Leave to soak in warm or hot water, not cold – and do this after the food has been served for easier washing up later.

❖ Always remove the pot from the outer casing before grilling or baking – and don't try these methods at all on a slow cooker with a fixed pot!

❖ Don't put food or liquid into the metal inner lining of the outer casing.

Cleaning
A removable pot may be taken out of the casing and washed in a dishwasher or in a bowl of hot soapy water, using a nylon scrubber or brush. A slow cooker with fixed pot should not be immersed in the water but should be stood on the draining board. Remove the flex, if detachable, otherwise keep the plug

well away from the water. Half fill with hot soapy water and clean using a nylon scrubber or brush. Pour away this water, fill with clean rinsing water, pour away and dry.

If a white chalky deposit marks the pot after steaming a pudding, remove it with a nylon, not metal, scourer and a mild liquid abrasive cleaner.

Wipe the exterior with a damp cloth. The inner lining may also be wiped if the pot is removable, but remember that the metal may still be hot. Take care not to let food spill out of the pot into the inner lining as it will burn on. Never put water into the outer casing.

Never try to repair an electrical fault yourself. The manufacturer is best equipped to do the job safely and efficiently.

27

Slow Cooking Techniques

SOUPS

Families large or small welcome the taste of home-made soups which can be made so conveniently and economically in a slow cooker.

Prepare soups from whatever is to hand. Eat it now or freeze all or part for another time. Don't discard vegetable peelings, bones or poultry carcasses as a matter of course. Instead make up a stock and you will have an excellent basis for future soups or casseroles which has cost virtually nothing.

Soups can be cooked all day or overnight as they generally need at least 8 hours cooking on LOW and most soups can be left for 12 hours without danger of overcooking. Soups usually involve lengthy preparation therefore you may find it more convenient to cut up the ingredients during the evening and cook through the night. Alternatively, the ingredients may be prepared the previous evening and the peelings, trimmings or bones may be cooked overnight as a stock for the next day's soup. This way a more delicate soup is not overpowered by the taste of a stronger flavoured stock cube.

To prepare a large quantity of soup in a smaller capacity slow cooker, simply double the solid ingredients and cook with the normal quantity of liquid. The cooking time will be the same. The soup may be frozen in this condensed form and diluted when re-heating. Freeze in single or double portions for quick re-heating in a saucepan.

To convert your own recipes, follow the basic method given below.

1. Pre-heat the slow cooker if necessary.

2. Assemble the ingredients and prepare as usual. Remember that root vegetables should be cut into 5mm/¼ in dice.

3. In a large saucepan fry the vegetables in a little fat or oil until softened but not browned. If you are following a low fat diet simply put the vegetables into the pan without pre-frying.

4. Add any meat and brown quickly on all sides. For a low fat diet, put the meat into the pan with the vegetables.

5. For 4-6 servings add approximately 1 litre/2 pints water or stock.

6. If you prefer a thickened soup, blend 1-2 tablespoonfuls of cornflour with sufficient water to make a cream-like consistency. Pour slowly into the pan and bring to the boil, stirring continuously until thickened.

7. If the soup has not to be thickened and ingredients have not been browned or sautéed, simply bring everything to the boil in the pan. Use a slotted spoon to remove any scum from the surface.

8. Add herbs and seasoning. For 1 litre/2 pints of stock made with a cube, use 2 teaspoonfuls of salt or to taste.

9. Transfer to the slow cooker and cook on LOW for 8-12 hours or on HIGH for 4-6 hours.

10. Cut from the bones any remaining meat and discard the bones. Adjust seasoning if necessary.

11. Some soups are improved by sieving or liquidising but you may prefer a chunky texture – the choice is yours. If a soup is liquidised it should be returned to the slow

cooker and re-heated on HIGH for 15 minutes. Alternatively, re-heat in a saucepan.

12. Soups can be made more luxurious by stirring in extras at the end of cooking. Fifteen minutes before serving stir in a beaten egg yolk, cream or milk. Do not add earlier as it could curdle. A garnish only takes a few minutes and makes soups more appealing. Just before serving, swirl in double cream, soured cream or natural yoghurt. Alternatively, sprinkle with one of the following: chopped fresh parsley, snipped fresh chives, chopped spring onions, grated cheese, fried bread croûtons, crumbled crisply fried bacon.

MEAT

Roasts

Meat or poultry roasted in the slow cooker is not as crisp as when cooked in an oven as the oven's high, dry heat cannot be reproduced. Nevertheless, slow cooked roasts are deliciously succulent. Buy a joint or bird which will fit in the pot and allow the lid to fit snugly. Trim excess fat and brown evenly on all sides in a frypan. With a non-stick pan it is possible to brown without adding further fat. Transfer to the slow cooker and season. Fattier meat may be stood on a trivet or crumpled foil. There is no need to add any liquid. Cook steamed puddings, joints of pork and whole birds on HIGH only to ensure thorough heat penetration. Casseroles of *cubed* pork or bird and portions of bird may be cooked on HIGH or LOW as wished.

After roasting, remove the meat to a hot serving dish and carefully pour the juices from the slow cooker into a jug. Allow it to settle for a moment and the fat will float to the top. Skim or pour off and strain the juices to make a delicious gravy.

Roasting times will depend on the size and shape of the meat and the proportion of fat and bone, but the following table can be a guide.

GUIDE TO ROASTING TIMES			
Meat	**Weight**	**Setting**	**Time**
Beef, lamb and veal	1-1.6kg (2-3½ lb)	LOW	4-10 hours
		HIGH	3-6 hours
	1.6-2.3kg (3½-5 lb)	LOW	7-12 hours
		HIGH	5-8 hours
Pork	1-1.6kg (2-3½ lb)	HIGH	3-5 hours
	1.6-2.3kg (3½-5 lb)	HIGH	4-6 hours
Chicken	1.5kg (3 lb)	HIGH	3½-4 hours
Duck	1.8kg (4 lb)	HIGH	5-6 hours
Pheasant	Large	HIGH	3-4 hours

Portions

If you want to cook a recipe to serve fewer people than is suggested, reduce the given quantities proportionately, always ensuring that the root vegetables are immersed. Less than two portions do not cook satisfactorily in larger slow cookers.

When increasing quantities to almost brim full in larger slow cookers, it is important to ensure that the heat can penetrate the mass of food in a casserole-type recipe. Consequently, if using the Browning method and hot stock, you may cook on LOW or HIGH setting as wished, but if using the One-Step method, you must add hot liquid at the beginning and cook only on HIGH throughout.

FISH

When cooking fish using conventional methods, care should be taken not to overcook the fish otherwise it will dry up or fall apart. With a slow cooker there is no need to time cooking to the minute. Nevertheless, fish will not cook successfully all day, even in a slow cooker, as its texture will toughen. Consequently cooking times are comparatively shorter than those needed for meat. However, a few hours away from the kitchen can be gained and, what's more, the water seal around the rim traps in the smell of cooking fish.

Use the following basic methods when slow cooking fish.

Baking fish
This is best for steaks or whole fish such as trout.

1.   Grease the stoneware pot and pre-heat if wished.

2.   Clean and dry the fish. Remove the head and tail if necessary so that the fish fits easily into the slow cooker.

3.   Put into the slow cooker and dot with butter.

4.   Cook steaks for 3-4 hours on LOW or 1-2 hours on HIGH.
     Cook *whole* fish for 4-6 hours on LOW or 2-3 hours on HIGH.

Poaching fish
1.   Grease the stoneware pot and pre-heat if wished.

2.   Clean and dry the fish. Remove the head and tail, if necessary, to fit the fish easily into the slow cooker.

3.   Place in the slow cooker and sprinkle with seasoning and flavourings. These may be herbs, finely chopped onion, grated lemon or orange rind.

4.   Pour over the fish sufficient liquid to half cover. This may be water, fish stock, water and vinegar, cider, beer, wine or fruit juice. Milk should be added at the end of cooking to avoid curdling.

5.   Cook for 3-4 hours on LOW or 1-2 hours on HIGH.

6.   Fish to be eaten cold should be transferred to a dish to cool in the liquor.

Casseroling fish
1.   Grease the stoneware pot and pre-heat if wished.

2.   Clean and dry the fish. Cut to size and put into the slow cooker.

3. In a frypan, gently fry in oil or butter vegetables such as onions, peppers, celery, root vegetables, etc., until softened but not browned. *Remember*: vegetables other than tomatoes need to be thinly sliced or diced when cooked with fish, otherwise they will need longer cooking and the fish could spoil.

4. Season the vegetables and add herbs if wished.

5. Pour 300ml (½ pint) liquid into the frypan. The liquid may be as suggested for poaching.

6. To thicken the casserole, blend 1 tablespoonful of cornflour with a little water and pour into the pan. Bring to the boil, stirring continuously until thickened. Pour the sauce over the fish.

7. Cook for 2-5 hours on LOW or 1-2 hours on HIGH.

VEGETABLES

Use your slow cooker for vegetables which would easily overcook with normal cooking. Ratatouille, for example, is a luxurious French vegetable stew which can all too easily become an indescribable mush if not carefully watched yet in the slow cooker each slice of courgette and aubergine retains its shape and the flavours develop to the full.

Vegetables are used more and more as a main course and it is so easy to slow cook stuffed vegetables which in the oven tend to collapse if cooked only a few minutes too long.

Although a slow cooker is ideal for the more delicate vegetables, it retains the flavour of all vegetables. The tougher vegetables can create problems however and root vegetables such as carrots and potatoes take much longer to cook than you would imagine. As mentioned earlier, they need longer cooking than meat, consequently they should be sliced thinly or diced small. Keep to 5mm/¼ in for the following: carrots, parsnips, potatoes, swedes, turnips, celery, onions, leeks, courgettes.

Cooking can be accelerated if these vegetables are gently sautéed in oil or butter before slow cooking. Alternatively they may be brought to the boil in a pan before being transferred to the slow cooker.

Carrots need the longest cooking because of their composition. Good results will not be achieved with either carrots or potatoes if they are cooked from absolutely cold.

Fresh vegetables should not be cooked as in a saucepan. The slow cooker does not boil and a quantity of prepared vegetables covered with boiling water and cooked in the slow cooker will not give a satisfactory result. The slow cooker is more suitable for vegetable casseroles or for baking stuffed vegetables.

Casseroling vegetables

1. Peel and cut the vegetables to size (5mm/¼ in for vegetables listed above).

2. Sauté the vegetables in oil or butter in a large frypan or saucepan. For a low fat diet simply place in a pan.

3. Sprinkle with seasoning and herbs.

4. Pour over sufficient liquid barely to cover the vegetables. Remember, however, that vegetables produce their own liquids during cooking and you will end up with too much liquid if you aren't careful. Nevertheless, the vegetables listed won't cook if not immersed and potatoes will also blacken if exposed.

5. Bring to the boil and transfer to the slow cooker.

6. Casseroles containing any of the listed vegetables should be cooked on LOW for 6-10 hours and on HIGH for 3-5 hours.

Potatoes

You may prefer to eat potatoes whole rather than cut small in a stew and it is possible to cook them whole in the slow cooker. The secret is aluminium foil. Peel and individually wrap each potato in a little parcel of foil and place them on top of the food in the casserole. The foil concentrates the heat and the whole potato cooks through in the 6-10 hours needed for most casseroles.

PUDDINGS

Surprisingly, slow cooking excels when it comes to puddings and desserts. Use your slow cooker to steam the lightest, moist sponge or suet puddings – without filling the kitchen with steam for hours at a time.

Fruit, which normally needs careful attention when cooking, retains its shape and texture in a slow cooker for use in flans and pies or as a refreshing chilled dessert.

Steamed pudding

1. Pre-heat the slow cooker on HIGH during the preparation.

2. Use a container which fits easily into the slow cooker and cover it with greased greaseproof paper or aluminium foil.

3. Use the lifting strap described on page 180 to lower the basin into the slow cooker.

4. Surround the container with sufficient boiling water to reach half-way up the side.

5. Steamed puddings containing a raising agent must be cooked on HIGH throughout to ensure a good rise. Do not exceed 3-4 hours cooking time otherwise the pudding will become dry.

Poached fruit

1. Switch on the slow cooker and pour in 550ml/1 pint boiling water. Stir in the sugar until dissolved. The quantity of sugar depends on taste and the natural sweetness of the fruit.

2. Prepare the fruit as normal and slice or leave whole.

3. Arrange the fruit in the slow cooker and ensure that apples are immersed during cooking otherwise they will discolour.

4. Cook on LOW or HIGH. Times will depend on the size and ripeness of the fruit.

GUIDE FOR COOKING FRUIT		
Fruit	**Setting**	**Time**
Apples, pears,		
whole	LOW	5-10 hours
sliced	LOW	3-5 hours
Berry fruits	LOW	2-5 hours

5.   If the stoneware pot is removable you may wish to cover the cooked fruit with crumble, pastry or meringue which can be cooked in the oven.

MISCELLANEOUS

There are other things which will cook successfully in a slow cooker and as you experiment you will discover more and more.

❖   *Pâté* can be cooked in a container surrounded by a water bath. Always cook on HIGH.

❖   *Lemon curd* cooks with no need to stir – and it doesn't curdle.

❖   *Cheese fondue* and *hot dips* can be cooked in and served from the slow cooker.

❖   *Fruit* for jams and marmalades can be softened in the slow cooker before fast boiling in a pan to reach setting point.

❖   *Punch* and *mulled wine* can be heated in and served from the slow cooker.

❖   *Hot dogs* and *herb bread* can be heated and kept hot in the slow cooker.

❖   *Cakes* and *tea-breads* may be cooked in a cake tin. Cover the tin tightly with aluminium foil, allowing room for the cake to rise. Surround with boiling water like a steamed pudding and cook only on HIGH. Cakes should never be cooked without adding water. The result is not as crisp or brown as when oven-baked, but icing or a jam glaze can disguise the fact. Chocolate cakes look attractive even without icing.

28

Recipes

BROCCOLI SOUP

Serves 4-6   *LOW 6-10 hours*

25g/1 oz butter or margarine
1 onion, finely chopped
450g/1 lb broccoli
850ml/1½ pints chicken stock
2 tsp salt
pepper
½ tsp nutmeg
small can evaporated milk

1. In a large saucepan gently sauté the onion in the butter or margarine.

2. Add the broccoli, stirring to mix with the onion.

3. Add the stock and seasoning and bring to the boil.

4. Transfer to the slow cooker and cook on LOW for 6-10 hours.

5. After cooking, liquidise or sieve and stir in the milk. Re-heat, without boiling, in a saucepan.

BRISKET IN A POT

Serves 4-6   *LOW 8-10 hours*

A meal in one pot. The size of your slow cooker will dictate the size of brisket and the amount of vegetables. The quantity given fits easily into a 3.5 litre/6 pint slow cooker, so reduce the amount of potatoes and carrots if using a smaller size. Remember that the root vegetables must be immersed in the stock for even cooking.

1.5kg/3 lb brisket of beef
salt and pepper
2 onions, sliced
6 carrots, thinly sliced
1 small swede, diced small
700g/1½ lb potatoes, thinly sliced
2 tbsp fresh chives
1 litre/2 pints boiling stock

1. Trim excess fat from the brisket and brown evenly on all sides in a non-stick frypan, without adding any fat, if possible. Season. Transfer to the slow cooker.

2. Add the vegetables, packing them around the sides of the brisket. Add 2 tsp salt and some pepper, the chives and boiling stock, ensuring that the vegetables are immersed in the stock. If necessary, increase the amount of stock to do so.

3. Cook for 8-10 hours on LOW.

Tip: If, after cooking, a great deal of broth is left, serve it as soup either before the meal or on another occasion.

MIDDLE EASTERN LAMB

Serves 4   *LOW 8-10 hours*

1kg/2 lb middle neck of lamb
1 onion, finely chopped
1 tbsp flour
1 tsp cumin
1 tsp turmeric
1 tsp salt
pepper
450ml/¾ pint stock
50g/2 oz red lentils
25g/1 oz stoned raisins
25g/1 oz chopped dates
1 tbsp lemon juice

1. In a non-stick frypan, fry the lamb without additional fat until browned on all sides. Transfer to the slow cooker.

2. In the fat left by the lamb, brown the onion.

3. Stir in the flour, cumin, turmeric, salt and pepper.

4. Add the stock gradually, stirring over a medium heat until the sauce thickens.

5. Add the remaining ingredients and bring to the boil.

6. Pour over the lamb, ensuring that the lentils are immersed in the sauce. Cook for 8-10 hours on LOW.

CHICKEN AND MUSHROOM CASSEROLE

Serves 4   *LOW 4-8 hours*

4 chicken quarters
1 tbsp flour
25g/1 oz butter or margarine
1 onion, finely chopped
2 sticks celery, thinly sliced
225g/8 oz mushrooms, thinly sliced
1 clove garlic, crushed (optional)
300ml/½ pint chicken stock
1 tsp salt
pepper
3 tbsp cream (optional)

1. Toss the chicken in the flour and fry in the butter or margarine until golden brown on all sides. Transfer to the slow cooker.

2. In the remaining fat, gently fry the onion and celery until softened but not browned.

3. Add the mushrooms and garlic (if using) and stir in the stock.

4. Bring to the boil, season and pour over the chicken. Ensure that the vegetables are immersed. It doesn't matter if the chicken isn't completely covered by the sauce.

5. Cook for 4-8 hours on LOW.

6. Before serving, stir in the cream (if using).

TROUT AND ALMONDS

Serves 4   *LOW 4-10 hours*

4 trout
salt and pepper
50g/2 oz flaked almonds
50g/2 oz butter

1. Butter the stoneware pot.

2. Clean the trout and remove the heads and tails. (The tails may be left on if the stoneware pot is wide enough to allow the fish to lie flat.) Rinse and dry the fish.

3. Season the trout inside and out and place on the bottom of the slow cooker. Sprinkle with the almonds and dot with the butter.

4. Cook on LOW for 4-10 hours.

VEGETARIAN CURRY

Serves 4   *LOW 8-10 hours*

1 onion, finely chopped
1 small head of celery, thinly sliced
1 red pepper, roughly chopped
1 tbsp olive oil
100g/4 oz orange lentils
1 tbsp curry powder
1 tsp turmeric
1 tsp cumin
1 tsp dried chilli
2 tbsp chutney
397g/14 oz can tomatoes, including juice
300ml/½ pint water
bay leaf
1 tsp salt
1 tbsp lemon juice
2 tbsp tomato purée

1. In a large frypan, gently fry the onion, celery and red pepper in the oil, until softened but not browned.

2. Add all the remaining ingredients. Bring to the boil and transfer to the slow cooker. Cook for 8-10 hours on LOW.

3. Remove the bay leaf before serving.

STUFFED TOMATOES

Serves 4 as a starter   *LOW 2-5 hours*

Double the quantity if serving as a supper dish with creamy
mashed potatoes.

4 medium tomatoes
50g/2 oz streaky bacon, finely chopped
50g/2 oz mushrooms, finely chopped
1 clove garlic, crushed
25g/1 oz fresh white breadcrumbs
salt
black pepper
pinch of thyme

1. Slice the top off each tomato, using a sharp knife.
    Carefully scoop out the pulp with a spoon.

2. In a small pan, fry the bacon without fat until golden
    and starting to crisp.

3. Stir in the mushrooms and garlic and cook for a minute
    over a low heat.

4. Remove from the heat and mix in the breadcrumbs,
    seasoning and thyme. Spoon the mixture into the
    tomato shells. Stand each tomato in the slow cooker and
    cook for 2-5 hours on LOW.

SAVOURY RICE

2 rashers streaky bacon, chopped
15g/½ oz butter
1 small green pepper, de-seeded and diced
1 onion, finely chopped
2 sticks celery, thinly sliced
1 clove of garlic, crushed
175g/6 oz easy-cook long grain rice
550ml/1 pint chicken stock
1 tsp salt
black pepper
½ tsp rosemary

1. Gently fry the bacon in the butter until starting to brown.

2. Add the green pepper, onion, celery and garlic and cook until softened but not browned.

3. Stir in the rice and fry for a few minutes.

4. Add all the remaining ingredients and bring to the boil.

5. Stir well and transfer to the slow cooker.

6. Cook for 2-3 hours on LOW, if possible stirring towards the end of cooking.

TIPSY APRICOTS

Serves 4   *LOW 2-3 hours*

150ml/¼ pint water, boiling
50g/2 oz caster sugar
450g/1 lb fresh apricots
vanilla essence
2 tbsp gin
cream to serve

1. Put the water and caster sugar into the slow cooker and switch to HIGH.

2. Using a sharp knife, cut each apricot in half and remove the stone.

3. Stir the sugar until dissolved and add the apricots, cut side downwards. Add a few drops of vanilla essence.

4. Switch to LOW and cook for 2-3 hours on LOW.

5. Transfer to a serving dish, add the gin, allow to cool then chill.

6. Serve with whipped cream.

GOLDEN LEMON PUDDING

Serves 4-6   *HIGH 3-4 hours*

100g/4 oz margarine
50g/2 oz caster sugar
2 tbsp golden syrup
50g/2 oz chopped mixed nuts
2 tbsp lemon juice
grated rind of 1 lemon
2 eggs, size 3, beaten
225g/8 oz self-raising flour

1. Pre-heat the slow cooker on HIGH while preparing the ingredients. Butter a 1 litre/2 pint pudding basin.

2. Put all the ingredients into a large bowl one at a time and beat together.

3. Spoon into the pudding basin and cover securely with aluminium foil. Using the lifting strap (see page 180), lower the basin into the slow cooker. Surround with sufficient boiling water to come halfway up the side of the basin. Cook on HIGH for 3-4 hours.

DATE AND WALNUT PUDDING

Serves 4   *HIGH 3-4 hours*

50g/2 oz butter or margarine
50g/2 oz caster sugar
1 egg, beaten
75g/3 oz self-raising flour
25g/1 oz dates, finely chopped
25g/1 oz walnuts, chopped
1 tbsp milk

1. Pre-heat the slow cooker on HIGH. Butter a 550ml/1 pint pudding basin.

2. Cream together the butter or margarine and sugar until pale and fluffy.

3. Beat in the egg and fold in half the flour and all the dates and walnuts.

4. Add the remaining flour, using the milk to give a good consistency.

5. Put the mixture into the pudding basin and cover tightly with greased greaseproof paper or aluminium foil. Using the lifting strap (see page 180), lower the basin into the slow cooker. Pour around sufficient boiling water to come halfway up the side of the basin. Cook on HIGH for 3-4 hours.

6. Unmould to serve.

Pressure
Cooking

29

Pressure Cookers

Pressure cooking explained in brief

When cooking in a saucepan, heat is lost as steam escapes from under the lid. A pressure cooker's lid fits so closely that an airtight seal is formed, trapping in the steam and allowing pressure to build up inside.

When water boils in a saucepan it is impossible for it to become hotter than boiling point (100°C). If water is heated under pressure, it *is* possible to increase that temperature and therefore cook the food more quickly.

Today's popular pressure cookers operate at three different pressures: LOW (5 lb per square inch), MEDIUM (10 lb per square inch) and HIGH (15 lb per square inch) pressure. At LOW pressure, water reaches 109°C; at MEDIUM 115°C; and at HIGH 121°C. Since most food is usually pressure cooked at HIGH pressure, you can appreciate how that extra 21°C helps to speed up cooking significantly.

Advantages of pressure cooking

Speedy

If you have never used a pressure cooker before, you will be amazed at the short cooking times. Cooking under pressure generally takes roughly one quarter to one third of the conventional cooking time. In some recipes the time saving is even greater and can be quicker than in a microwave. For example, a beef stew that normally takes 1½ hours to cook conventionally can be pressure cooked in 15-20 minutes.

The speed of pressure cooking means that those traditional well-loved recipes, often neglected because they need hours of cooking or close attention, can be prepared quickly and easily. Dried pulses (peas and beans) can be cooked in a fraction of the normal time too.

Economical
The shorter cooking times inevitably result in fuel savings. Remember too that, once the required cooking pressure has been reached, the heat is usually turned down to minimum setting for the remainder of the cooking time.

Even greater savings can be made if you cook more than one kind of food in the pressure cooker at the same time – a great advantage if you cook mainly for one or two, or if you are keen to economise. A main course and vegetables can be cooked together, with a dessert included for good measure. The secret is to choose food with similar cooking times or to adjust the preparation of food so that it all cooks in the same time. For example, with chops you can use root vegetables which are unlikely to overcook in the time it takes for the meat to cook but with fish any accompanying potatoes would need to be thinly sliced to ensure they are fully cooked.

Pressure cooking can be economical when cooking for crowds too, or when bulk cooking for the freezer. It is often worthwhile cooking double the amount you need and freezing half. Remember that increasing the quantity of ingredients (particularly in soups and stews) does not usually result in a longer pressure cooking time. The time only needs adjusting if you increase the size of foods such as meat joints or steamed puddings. The main point to remember is never to over-fill the pressure cooker.

Savings don't stop with fuel either. A pressure cooker will quickly cook cheaper cuts of meat – the ones that are packed with flavour but normally need long slow cooking to make them tender. Dried beans, usually a cheap source of protein, can be pressure cooked in just 20 minutes.

Improved flavour, colour and nutrition

We all recognise the welcoming aroma of a delicious casserole bubbling away gently in the oven or on the hob, but it's easy to forget that, along with the steam, some of the flavour is also escaping. A pressure cooker is designed to seal in the steam and, as a result, retain most of the flavour.

Pressure cooking also helps to prevent the loss of colour that occurs in long, slow cooking – particularly in vegetables.

No matter how food is cooked, it's inevitable that a certain amount of nutritional value will be lost. Nevertheless, the short cooking times in a pressure cooker, combined with the small quantity of liquid and the absence of light and air, help to retain vitamins and minerals which might normally be lost.

Less steam and reduced cooking smells

A pressure cooker allows only a small amount of steam to escape, which enables you to cook steamed puddings and stews without the windows running with condensation. Cooking smells in the kitchen are thus reduced too.

A boon for camping, caravanning and boating

A pressure cooker is invaluable on self-catering holidays where time and space for cooking are at a premium.

Choosing a pressure cooker

All pressure cookers work on the basic principle described above. How they usually differ is in the way they operate. Some pressure cookers have a choice of three different pressures (see above), some have two, while some older models have only one fixed pressure.

A pressure cooker with a choice of three pressures is very versatile and will cook a wide variety of food. For example, LOW (5 lb) pressure is ideal for cooking a pudding that contains a raising agent (this ensures that the pudding rises before it 'sets') or for bottling fruit. MEDIUM (10 lb) pressure is recommended for softening fruit for jam or jelly making. HIGH (15 lb) pressure is ideal for everyday cooking of soups, vegetables and casserole-type dishes.

Fig. 22. A typical pressure cooker with weight. Some models offer a choice of three pressures while others have two.

Pressure cookers that have two pressures usually cook at 6 lb and 12 lb. This means that cooking temperatures are a little lower and cooking times are slightly longer.

Pressure cookers with a single fixed pressure tend to operate at just 7½ lb. Again, this means that cooking temperatures are lower and cooking times are longer. At 7½ lb pressure, recipes that recommend HIGH (15 lb) need twice the cooking time.

Before buying a pressure cooker, decide which size you need. Even the smaller models will cook a stew for four people but might not be large enough for a big joint of meat, bulk cooking for the freezer or for fruit bottling. On the one hand, pressure cookers can last 20-25 years, so it might be worth looking ahead and planning for the future when you buy. On the other hand, do not be tempted to choose the largest pressure cooker you can find if you don't cook in large quantities on a regular basis. Remember, too, that you will need a convenient place to store it.

Assess the weight of the pressure cooker by lifting it and imagining it with the additional weight of the food. Make

sure the pressure cooker has a thick base because, as you will
see later in the book, it needs to withstand sudden drops in
temperature when it is taken hot from the hob to stand in a
bowl of cold water to reduce pressure. Without a sturdy base,
in time, the bottom of the pressure cooker might bow, causing
the pressure cooker to become inefficient.

In some models, a clockwork timer activates an automatic
pressure-reducing device at the end of the chosen cooking
time (you will need to remember to switch off the heat
immediately, otherwise the cooker would eventually boil dry).

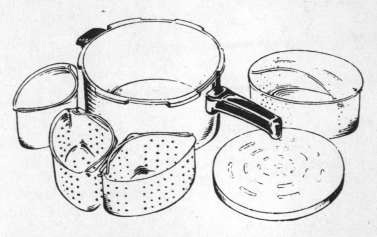

Fig. 23. Typical pressure cooker accessories can include (from left to
right): an unperforated basket, perforated baskets, trivet and blanching basket.

Accessories vary from model to model but basically every
pressure cooker has a removable rack or trivet, which is used
to hold food that is to be steam cooked above the water level
(necessary with vegetables, for example, particularly when
more than one type is cooked at the same time). Baskets are
often supplied and these are designed to keep foods separate
so that their different flavours do not intermingle. The baskets
are usually perforated to allow the steam to circulate. Sometimes, an unperforated basket is provided for cooking food

such as egg custards, rice or stewed apple. Additional accessories might include separators or a basket for blanching vegetables for the freezer.

Finally, please have no fears about the safety of today's pressure cookers. Those made by reputable manufacturers have been perfected over the years and are utterly safe to use. They are fitted with several devices, each designed to release pressure in the unlikely event that a vent becomes blocked or the pressure cooker has been allowed to boil dry and overheat.

Make sure your model has a well-written instruction book from the manufacturer.

30

Using a Pressure Cooker

Before using a pressure cooker for the first time, read the manufacturer's instruction book carefully – it will tell you all you need to know about its operation (an obvious point but important nonetheless). In the meantime, here is a brief outline of how to use one.

A pressure cooker must contain a small amount of liquid in order to produce the steam to raise the pressure. The longer the cooking time, the more liquid is needed. Generally, the minimum recommended by manufacturers for cooking times up to 30 minutes is 300ml/½ pint. This liquid can be water, stock, beer, cider, wine, soup, or any combination of these. (Do not attempt to use oil as the cooking liquid – it's dangerous because it cannot create steam.) It is important to use the correct amount of liquid recommended for the recipe – too little could cause the pressure cooker to boil dry and overheat.

When cooking soups or casseroles, the trivet isn't needed as the flavours should intermingle during cooking. Some recipes require vegetables and meat to be softened or browned first and this can be done in the open base of the pressure cooker before adding the liquid and remaining ingredients. When you use the trivet, it is a good idea to put the water into the pressure cooker first – the water can't always be seen below the trivet and this way you avoid the risk of forgetting to add it.

Remember that for the food to cook there must be room for the steam to circulate. Do not fill the pressure cooker more than two thirds full of solid food such as vegetables. With recipes that contain a lot of liquid and are likely to froth up (such as soups, casseroles, milk puddings, rice and jam), the pressure cooker should not be filled more than half full.

After adding the ingredients to the pressure cooker, fit the lid carefully, making sure that it is locked tightly in position before allowing the pressure to rise. For pressure cookers with long, saucepan-type handles this means that the lid handle should lie directly over the base handle.

Once the lid is in position, the pressure cooker can be brought to pressure. The method depends on the type of pressure cooker.

1. Visual pressure indicator

The visual pressure indicator weight is a neat device which contains a plunger that rises and falls as the pressure rises and falls. It is marked with two or three rings and, as each ring appears, it shows which pressure has been reached.

When the lid has been fitted and the heat is turned on under the pressure cooker, the liquid inside it heats up. As it boils, it creates steam, which causes the pressure (and the plunger) to rise. As soon as the plunger shows the correct number of rings, the heat is turned down so that the plunger remains steady (without any hissing or spluttering) and pressure is maintained. If it does hiss and splutter, it means that the heat is too high. If you are already using minimum heat, you may need to move the pressure cooker gently half way off the ring (this is particularly relevant to electric hobs with solid and radiant plates). If the heat has been turned down too low, the pressure will drop and the plunger will fall slightly. Simply increase the heat a little until you have found the correct heat to maintain pressure.

2. Audible pressure indicator

This type indicates when pressure is reached by the noise it makes. The weight usually consists of three parts that are screwed together for cooking at three different pressures.

Fig. 24. A visual pressure indicator weight, in which a plunger rises and falls as the pressure inside the pressure cooker rises and falls.

After fitting the lid, the weight is clicked on to the central vent, the heat is turned on, the liquid inside boils and the pressure rises. As this happens, the pressure cooker will start to hiss slightly. As soon as you hear a louder hissing sound this means that pressure has been reached and the heat should be reduced until only a gentle mutter can be heard. As with the previous type of pressure weight, it may be necessary to draw the pressure cooker slightly off a solid or radiant electric ring to maintain the correct sound. If the pressure cooker becomes silent, it means that the pressure has dropped too far and the heat should be increased slightly.

Fig. 25. An audible pressure indicator weight usually consists of three parts that are screwed together for cooking at different pressures.

3. Fixed pressure valve

This type has a valve that rotates (or spins) when pressure is reached and usually operates at one pressure. Once the lid is in position, the valve is positioned on the air vent. The heat is turned on and, as the liquid inside boils, so pressure increases. As soon as the valve starts to spin, the heat should be reduced until it stops rotating.

No matter which type of pressure cooker you use, the cooking time is calculated from the moment pressure is reached – from the moment when the plunger shows the required ring, or when the pressure cooker starts to hiss loudly, or when the rotating valve starts to spin. How long it takes to reach pressure depends largely on what is inside the pressure cooker. If it contains only a few potatoes and carrots with 300ml/½ pint water, it won't take long. If, on the other hand, 1.2 litres/2 pints of stock is to be brought to the boil, it will take longer. It is important not to exceed the cooking times because delicate foods can easily overcook.

At the end of the cooking time, the pressure can be reduced in one of two ways.

❖　*To reduce the pressure quickly:*
Stand the pressure cooker in a bowl of cold water. Use this method for food which is likely to spoil if over-cooked and for food that is cooked in only a small amount of liquid.

❖　*To reduce the pressure slowly at room temperature:*
Turn off the heat, gently move the pressure cooker to a cold part of the hob (or stand it on a wooden chopping board or heat-resistant surface) and leave it to cool. Use this method for foods that are likely to froth up a lot during pressure cooking – such as soups, rice or dried beans and peas.

With the visual pressure indicator, the plunger drops down and the automatic air vent in the lid falls as the pressure reduces.

With the audible pressure indicator, wait until it is silent then, using a fork, tip the weight slightly and, if no steam escapes, lift it off.

With the fixed pressure valve, reduce pressure by lifting the rotating valve slightly to release the steam.

Looking after your pressure cooker

Each time you use your pressure cooker, check that the vent pipe and other safety devices are clean and free to operate.

After use, wash the pressure cooker parts in hot, soapy water, rinse and dry. Check your manufacturer's instruction book because some parts may not be suitable for immersing in water.

The rubber-like gasket may shrink slightly after a considerable time and so it is a good idea to stretch it (gently) occasionally while it is cold. If, in time, steam starts to escape from under the lid, it probably means that the gasket needs replacing. This, along with other spare parts, can be obtained direct from the manufacturer if you can't find them at a local shop.

Store the pressure cooker with its lid upside down on the base (you may like to put a cloth between them to prevent scratching). This way, there is no stress on the gasket and all the parts will be well ventilated. If the weight is separate from the lid, make sure it is kept somewhere safe where it can't be damaged.

Adapting recipes for pressure cooking

The easiest way is to refer to similar recipes in the manufacturer's instruction book, and follow the same method. If in doubt, work out which ingredient needs the longest cooking time and use that as your guide.

When the quantity of food is increased, it is only necessary to extend the cooking time if you are cooking a larger joint of meat or steamed pudding, in which case the heat has to penetrate a greater bulk.

The cooking time governs how much liquid is needed and manufacturers give instructions in their books. Remember that when pressure cooking stews and casseroles, there won't be as much evaporation as with conventional cooking, so you won't need quite so much liquid. All the same, don't forget to include at least the minimum amount of liquid recommended by the manufacturer.

Stews and meat dishes can be thickened slightly before cooking but use no more than 25g/1 oz flour, otherwise the steam may find it difficult to circulate adequately and the food may burn on the bottom. Stir the thickened dish well before pressure cooking to prevent food sticking. If further thickening is required, this should be done after cooking.

A word on freezing
When cooking in bulk for the freezer, bear in mind the following points:

❖ Garlic reduces the storage time to 1 month, so if you plan to freeze the food, simply omit the garlic.

❖ Do not thicken before freezing – it is best done after reheating, using cornflour blended to a smooth paste with a little liquid.

❖ Freeze in single or double portions for convenience.

❖ If food is to be reheated from frozen in the pressure cooker, freeze in shallow containers of a size that will fit inside the pressure cooker.

❖ To reheat, put 150ml/¼ pint water in the pressure cooker, without the trivet. Remove the portions from their containers and place in the water. Fit the lid and bring to pressure. The reheating time will depend on the size of the portion but, as a general rule, cook for 20 minutes at HIGH pressure. Reduce the pressure slowly at room temperature. If wished, thicken before serving. If foil containers are used to contain the frozen food, these may be stood on the trivet over 300ml/½ pint water and pressure cooked for 20 minutes at HIGH pressure.

❖ All frozen poultry and game must be completely thawed before pressure cooking.

❖ When reheating cooked recipes from frozen, make sure that the food is piping hot before serving.

❖ There is no need to thaw frozen fish before cooking, unless it is to be stuffed. Cooking times are the same as for fresh fish.

31

Cooking with Pressure

SOUPS

Soup making, like bread making and growing your own vegetables, has become very popular over the years. Why do people bother? If you've tasted bread fresh from the oven and beans fresh from the garden you will understand why people take the trouble to make their own soup. But is it trouble? Certainly not with a pressure cooker.

When making soup in a saucepan, the preparation and finishing off are often the shortest parts of the whole process. It's the long simmering that takes the time and ties you to the kitchen. With a pressure cooker, soups can be ready in minutes.

Once you have tried home-made soup you will be reluctant to use tins or packets again. Furthermore, you will become Scrooge-like about leftovers and vegetable peelings. Well washed peelings make an ideal base for a soup so don't waste their goodness.

When a recipe calls for stock, don't automatically turn to a stock cube. With your pressure cooker you can prepare real stock in 30-40 minutes. Apart from a rather smug feeling of cooking 'properly', there is no doubt that the flavour is much better, especially for more delicately flavoured dishes.

Here are some guidelines for adapting favourite recipes to pressure cooking:

❖ Don't use the trivet when making soup or stock as the idea is to mingle all the flavours together in the liquid.

❖ Don't fill the pressure cooker more than half full of liquid as it needs to boil up when cooking – you can always add more liquid at the end of the cooking time and bring the soup to the boil again in the open pressure cooker.

❖ When reducing pressure, do this slowly at room temperature. Simply switch off the heat and gently move the pressure cooker to a cool part of the hob.

❖ When converting your own recipes, remember there is less evaporation with pressure cooking, so don't allow for the extra liquid which normally boils away. BUT always remember to use the minimum amount of liquid in your pressure cooker as recommended by your manufacturer's instructions – usually 300ml/½ pint.

❖ Season in moderation. It is always best to add more salt and pepper at the end of cooking rather than having to correct an over-salty soup.

❖ Always add thickening at the end of the cooking.

❖ When making a basic stock, more flavour is obtained from the bones if they are cut small, so ask your butcher to chop them for you. Ingredients not suitable for stock making include: green vegetables, milk, gravy, thickened sauces, bread and potatoes.

❖ When preparing soup for the freezer, remember the earlier point about not filling the pressure cooker above the half-way mark, then, instead of adding the extra liquid at the end of the cooking, it is a good idea to freeze the soup in its concentrated form as it takes up less space. Add the remaining liquid when thawing and re-heating.

❖ When calculating the cooking time for your own recipes, remember that this will be dictated by the ingredient that takes the longest to cook.

MEAT, POULTRY AND GAME

A pressure cooker is a boon for cooking meat. Not only is the cooking time less than with conventional methods, but the super-heated steam penetrates the meat to make it really tender. Very little steam escapes during pressure cooking, so all the flavour is trapped inside.

The fact that pressure cooking is a moist cooking method means that it's great for boiling, braising, casseroling, stewing and pot roasting.

Here are some guidelines for adapting your own recipes to pressure cooking:

❖ The trivet is not used when cooking stews or casseroles but may be used when pot roasting.

❖ Use HIGH pressure and, in general, reduce pressure quickly after cooking (unless the recipe uses a large quantity of liquid or recommends otherwise).

❖ Quantities can be increased but make sure the pressure cooker is no more than two thirds full.

❖ Time is influenced by the quality of the meat, its size and thickness. You will soon get a 'feel' for timing but use the recipes in your instruction book as a guide. When increasing quantities for stews or casseroles there is no need to increase the cooking time.

❖ Meat may be tossed in a tablespoon of seasoned flour before cooking to give a slightly thickened gravy, but if really thick stews are preferred, add extra thickening *after* pressure cooking, using flour or cornflour blended to a smooth paste with a little liquid. Too much thickening before cooking would restrict the amount of steam available for circulation, with the risk that food could stick to the base.

❖ Remember that there is less evaporation compared with oven or hob cooking. Consequently adapted recipes won't need more than the recommended minimum of liquid. As a general rule, this is 300ml/½ pint for the first 20 minutes and 150ml/¼ pint for each extra 15 minutes' cooking (check your instruction book too).

❖ When choosing a joint of meat or a bird for pot roasting, make sure that it will fit inside your pressure cooker without blocking any of the air vents. Joints over 1.35kg/3 lb are not really suitable for pressure cooking as the outside will over-cook before the centre is done.

For cooking Pot Roast, use the following table as a guide:

GUIDE TO COOKING TIMES AT HIGH PRESSURE FOR MEAT

Meat	450g/1 lb	900g/2 lb	1.35kg/3 lb
Beef, lamb, mutton, pork, veal	300ml/ ½ pint 15 minutes	425ml/ ¾ pint 30 minutes	600ml/ 1 pint 45 minutes
Bacon, ham	300ml/ ½ pint 12 minutes	300ml/ ½ pint 24 minutes	425ml/ ¾ pint 36 minutes

GUIDE TO COOKING TIMES AT HIGH PRESSURE FOR POULTRY AND GAME

Poultry and game may be stuffed but remember to weigh *after* stuffing when calculating the cooking time. Cooking times of joints will vary depending on the thickness of the joint.

Poultry or Game	Type of Joint	Cooking Time
Chicken	Poussin	4-7 minutes
	Roasting, whole	7 minutes per 450g/1 lb
	, joints	7-10 minutes
	Boiling, whole	10 minutes per 450g/1 lb
	, joints	15-20 minutes
Duckling	Whole	12-15 minutes per 450g/1 lb
	Joints	10-12 minutes

GUIDE TO COOKING TIMES AT HIGH PRESSURE FOR POULTRY AND GAME

Poultry or Game	Type of Joint	Cooking Time
Grouse	Young	10 minutes
	Old	15 minutes
Hare	Joints *Minimum 600ml/1 pint liquid required*	35-40 minutes
Rabbit	Joints	20-25 minutes
Partridge		7-10 minutes
Pheasant	Whole	7-10 minutes
Pigeons	Halved	20-25 minutes
Venison		20-25 minutes per 450g/ 1 lb

FISH

Time saving is not the big advantage when pressure cooking fish; indeed, conventional methods don't take much longer. The main advantage is that only the minimum liquid is usually required and this helps reduce loss of flavour. Furthermore, the smell of fish is trapped inside the pressure cooker until the end of cooking.

Most fish recipes are improved with the addition of a good home-made fish stock (see page 241).

The following methods can be adapted to pressure cooking:

Poaching

1. The trivet is not used.

2. Prepare the fish and place it in the pressure cooker.

3. Add a minimum of 300ml/½ pint liquid. This may be slightly salted water with a teaspoonful of lemon juice, or wine or cider. If the poaching liquid is to be used as the basis of a sauce, sliced vegetables and herbs can be

included to give extra flavour. A mixture of half milk to water is good for smoked fish with no salt added.

4.   Fit the lid and bring to HIGH pressure. Cook for the time recommended in the table.

5.   Reduce the pressure quickly in cold water.

6.   The fish may then be flaked and served in a sauce, pie, pancakes or pastry cases. If the fish is to be served cold, allow it to cool in the poaching liquor.

Steaming
1.   Use the trivet, which should be lightly greased to prevent the fish from sticking.

2.   Put a minimum of 300ml/½ pint water into the pressure cooker with the trivet. Make sure that the water level is no higher than the trivet.

3.   Prepare the fish and place it on the trivet. Sprinkle with lemon juice, salt and pepper.

4.   Fit the lid and bring to HIGH pressure. Cook for the time recommended in the table (see below).

5.   Reduce the pressure quickly in cold water.

En papillote (in a packet)
1.   Use the trivet.

2.   Prepare the fish and place it on a greased square of foil. It can be seasoned and dotted with butter, stuffed or sprinkled with finely sliced vegetables, such as onion, mushrooms or celery. The foil should then be folded over the fish and sealed to form a secure parcel.

3.   Put 300ml/½ pint water into the pressure cooker with the trivet.

4.   Place the parcel on the trivet, fit the lid and bring to HIGH pressure. Cook for the time recommended in the table (see opposite).

5.   Reduce the pressure quickly in cold water.

Stewing/Casseroling

1. The trivet is not used.

2. Prepare the fish and cut it into chunks.

3. An onion and other vegetables may be sautéed in butter or margarine in the open pressure cooker. As fish takes such a short time to pressure cook, ensure that root vegetables, such as potatoes and carrots are thinly sliced to cook within the allotted time.

4. Add the fish, some lemon juice and at least 300ml/ ½ pint stock, wine or cider. Add herbs and seasoning.

5. Fit the lid and bring to HIGH pressure. Cook for the time recommended in the table (see below).

6. Reduce the pressure quickly in cold water.

Braising

Follow the general method for stewing, except that the fish is cooked whole on the greased trivet, which is placed on top of the vegetables and raised above the liquid. The vegetables can be puréed afterwards to make a sauce.

GUIDE TO COOKING TIMES AT HIGH PRESSURE FOR FISH		
Times will vary depending on the thickness of the fish.		
Fish	**Steaks or Fillets**	**Whole**
Bass, bream, brill, cod, coley, haddock, hake, halibut, ling, monk-fish, plaice, skate, sole, turbot, whiting	3-6 minutes	5-6 minutes per 450g/1 lb
Herrings, mackerel, mullet, trout	3-6 minutes	5-8 minutes
Lobster		10 minutes
Crab		7-10 minutes
Prawns, shrimps		2-3 minutes

VEGETABLES AND RICE

Vegetables benefit from pressure cooking not only because it saves time, but also because it can reduce the loss of colour, flavour and vitamins which occurs when cooking in a pan of boiling water. The small amount of cooking water used can be added to flavour soups or gravy.

Rice can be cooked either as a plain accompaniment, to serve with curry or other oriental dishes, or together with vegetables, meat or fish as a complete dish.

Rice

1. Put 175g/6 oz long grain rice into an unperforated basket or container.

2. Add 600ml/1 pint salted water and cover securely with greaseproof paper or foil.

3. Put 300ml/½ pint water into the pressure cooker, with the trivet. Stand the container of rice on the trivet.

4. Fit the lid, bring to HIGH pressure and cook for 5 minutes.

5. Reduce the pressure slowly at room temperature.

6. Fluff the rice with a fork before serving.

All in together

A selection of vegetables can be pressure cooked simultaneously. Ideally they should have similar cooking times, otherwise the more delicate vegetables will overcook. If this is not possible, then cut the larger vegetables into smaller pieces to compensate. Medium-sized potatoes will cook in a similar time to whole carrots and parsnips. If you prefer your carrots sliced, then the other vegetables should be cut smaller. Mashed potatoes, carrots and runner beans can be cooked at the same time by finely slicing the potato, thinly slicing the carrots and leaving the beans in fairly large lengths.

Cooking times

Cooking times will depend on the size and quality of the vegetables (see below for a guide to cooking times). Remember, whole carrots take longer to cook than sliced; new potatoes need longer than old ones. Individual taste also varies, so if you prefer your vegetables with a 'bite', reduce the cooking times slightly.

Fresh vegetables

1. The trivet is used to keep the vegetables above the water. Use the minimum amount of liquid required – usually 300ml/½ pint or 150ml/¼ pint.

2. Prepare the vegetables, put them into the perforated baskets and stand them on the trivet. If a large quantity of one vegetable is being cooked, pile it straight on to the trivet, making sure the pressure cooker is no more than two thirds full.

3. Fit the lid and bring to HIGH pressure. Cook for the recommended time.

4. Reduce the pressure quickly in cold water.

GUIDE TO COOKING TIMES FOR VEGETABLES AT HIGH PRESSURE	
When pressure cooking frozen vegetables, there is no need to thaw them first. Cook for the time recommended for fresh vegetables as given here.	
Vegetable	**Cooking Time**
Artichokes, globe	6-10 minutes
Artichokes, Jerusalem	4-6 minutes
Asparagus	2-4 minutes
Beans, broad	3-5 minutes
Beans, French or runner	3-5 minutes
Beetroot, small	10 minutes
Beetroot, medium	15-20 minutes
Beetroot, large	20-30 minutes

GUIDE TO COOKING TIMES FOR VEGETABLES AT HIGH PRESSURE	
Broccoli	3-4 minutes
Brussels sprouts	3-4 minutes
Cabbage, shredded	3 minutes
Carrots, whole	6-7 minutes
Carrots, sliced	3-4 minutes
Cauliflower, whole	5-8 minutes
Cauliflower, florets	3-4 minutes
Celery	3 minutes
Chicory, whole	3-6 minutes
Courgettes, whole	3-4 minutes
Courgettes, sliced	1-2 minutes
Leeks, whole	4 minutes
Leeks, sliced	2 minutes
Marrow, thickly sliced	3-4 minutes
Onions, sliced	3 minutes
Onions, whole	6-10 minutes
Parsnips, quartered	5-7 minutes
Parsnips, sliced	4 minutes
Peas	3-4 minutes
Peppers, stuffed	5 minutes
Potatoes, new, small, whole	6-7 minutes
Potatoes, old, whole	12 minutes
Potatoes, old, quartered	7 minutes
Potatoes, old, sliced	5 minutes
Spinach	1-2 minutes
Swede, cubed	4 minutes
Sweetcorn, whole	3-5 minutes
Turnip, sliced	2-3 minutes

Dried beans and peas

1. With a pressure cooker, long overnight soaking is unnecessary. Lentils require no soaking at all and other vegetables need only one hour.

2. Wash the dried vegetables, cover with boiling water and leave to soak for an hour. Do not use bicarbonate of soda, as it may stain the pressure cooker.

3. The trivet is not required. Pour into the pressure cooker at least 1.2 litres/2 pints liquid, part of which can be made up from the soaking water. This quantity is sufficient for cooking 450g/1 lb of vegetables and should be increased proportionately if more vegetables are to be cooked.

4. Bring the liquid to the boil and add the drained vegetables. Don't fill the pressure cooker more than half full as the liquid tends to froth up during cooking.

5. Reduce the heat to medium, fit the lid and bring to HIGH pressure on this heat. Cook for the time recommended in the table below.

6. Reduce the pressure slowly at room temperature.

GUIDE TO COOKING TIMES AT HIGH PRESSURE FOR DRIED BEANS AND PEAS	
Dried Vegetable	**Cooking Time**
Butter beans	30 minutes
Borlotti and Haricot beans, small	20 minutes
Haricot beans, large	30 minutes
Red Kidney beans	20 minutes
Lentils	7 minutes
Peas, whole	20 minutes
Peas, split	15 minutes

Blanching vegetables for freezing

1. Blanching vegetables for freezing in a pressure cooker is quick, uses little fuel and reduces the steam in the kitchen. Instead of the large pan of boiling water usually needed, use only the minimum amount of liquid required – usually 300ml/½ pint or 150ml/¼ pint.

2. Prepare the vegetables for freezing, as normal.

3. Put the water into the pressure cooker, together with the trivet, and bring the water to the boil.

4. Pile the vegetables loosely into the perforated baskets or in a special blanching basket. Don't fill the pressure cooker more than two-thirds full or pack the vegetables too tightly, as this prevents full circulation of the steam.

5. Fit the lid and bring to MEDIUM pressure. Cook them for the times given in the table below. Do not exceed the recommended times or the vegetables will end up cooked rather than blanched.

6. Reduce the pressure quickly in cold water. Remove the vegetables and immediately plunge them into plenty of cold water to cool quickly. Drain, dry, pack and freeze as usual.

GUIDE TO BLANCHING TIMES AT MEDIUM PRESSURE	
Vegetable	**Cooking Time**
Artichokes, Jerusalem, cubed	1 minute
Asparagus	Bring to pressure only
Beans, broad	1 minute
Beans, French or runner	Bring to pressure only
Beetroot, sliced	7 minutes
Broccoli	1 minute
Brussels sprouts	1 minute
Carrots	2 minutes

GUIDE TO BLANCHING TIMES AT MEDIUM PRESSURE	
Vegetable	**Cooking Time**
Cauliflower, florets	1 minute
Celery, young hearts	2 minutes
Celery stalks	1 minute
Courgettes, sliced	Bring to pressure only
Chicory	1 minute
Parsnips, sliced	1 minute
Peas	1 minute
Potatoes, new, small	2 minutes
Spinach	Bring to pressure only
Swede, sliced	1 minute
Sweetcorn	2 minutes
Turnips, small, whole	2 minutes

PUDDINGS

Although a pressure cooker is excellent for steaming traditional sponge and suet puddings, it's also good at cooking more delicate desserts, such as Crème Caramel. If you wish to convert a favourite recipe to pressure cooking, follow these guidelines.

Fresh fruit

Ripeness and size
When selecting fruit for pressure cooking, remember that for best results the pieces should be of equal size with the same degree of ripeness. A small, ripe pear will fall apart before a larger, harder pear is cooked.

Purée
1. The trivet is not required when cooking fruit for a purée. In the open pressure cooker, dissolve 115g/4 oz

sugar in the minimum recommended amount of water (check your instruction book – usually 150ml/¼ pint or 300ml/½ pint).

2. Add the washed and roughly chopped fruit, making sure the pressure cooker is no more than half full (some fruit tends to froth up during pressure cooking).

3. Fit the lid and bring to pressure. Use HIGH pressure for most fruit. Rhubarb and apple are best cooked at MEDIUM pressure as they tend to froth during cooking. (See table opposite for cooking times.)

4. Reduce the pressure slowly at room temperature.

5. Sieve the fruit or blend in a processor or liquidiser.

Soft fruit

Cooking in a container best retains the shape of more delicate soft fruit. You need to add no liquid as it will produce its own concentrated juice. The container can be metal, ovenproof glass or china or boilable plastic. A soufflé dish is ideal as it can be used afterwards for serving at the table.

1. Arrange the washed and prepared fruit in layers in the container. Sprinkle sugar to taste between each layer. Cover securely with greaseproof paper or foil.

2. Put 300ml/½ pint water into the pressure cooker. Add the trivet and stand the container on it. Fit the lid and bring to HIGH pressure. Follow the table for approximate cooking times (bear in mind that a china or glass dish will add 3-4 minutes to the cooking time).

3. Reduce the pressure quickly in cold water.

Stone fruit

When cooking fruit with a stone, follow the method given for soft fruit. Either halve and stone the fruit or prick the skins twice with a fork.

GUIDE TO COOKING TIMES AT HIGH PRESSURE
FOR FRESH FRUIT

Fruit	Method	Purée	Container Method
Apples, sliced	For purée use MEDIUM pressure	3 minutes	5-7 minutes
Apples, whole	See Apples with Honeyed Fruit, page 248	–	–
Apricots, halved	For container method, add 2 tbsp water	3 minutes	5-7 minutes
Blackberries		3 minutes	5-7 minutes
Blackcurrants		3 minutes	5-7 minutes
Cherries	For container method, cook whole with 2 tbsp water	–	5-7 minutes
Damsons	For container method, add 2 tbsp water	3 minutes	5-7 minutes
Gooseberries		3 minutes	5-7 minutes
Greengages	For container method, add 2 tbsp water	3 minutes	5-7 minutes
Loganberries		1 minute	4-6 minutes
Pears	See Pears in Red Wine, page 249	3 minutes	–
Peaches, sliced		3 minutes	5-7 minutes
Peaches, halved	See Filled Peaches with Almonds, page 250	3 minutes	5-7 minutes
Plums	For container method, add 2 tbsp water	3 minutes	5-7 minutes

GUIDE TO COOKING TIMES AT HIGH PRESSURE FOR FRESH FRUIT			
Fruit	**Method**	**Purée**	**Container Method**
Raspberries		1 minute	4-6 minutes
Rhubarb	For purée use MEDIUM pressure	1 minute	5-7 minutes

Dried fruit

1. Wash the fruit in hot water and place in a bowl. Cover with boiling water, allowing 600ml/1 pint for each 450g/1 lb fruit. Cover and leave to soak for 10 minutes.

2. Drain and measure the soaking water, making sure that you have at least 300ml/$\frac{1}{2}$ pint to pour into the pressure cooker, without the trivet. Add the fruit with 2-3 table-spoonfuls of sugar, or to taste.

3. Fit the lid and bring to HIGH pressure. Follow the table below for cooking times.

4. Reduce the pressure slowly at room temperature.

GUIDE TO COOKING TIMES AT HIGH PRESSURE FOR DRIED FRUIT	
Fruit	**Cooking Time**
Apple rings	6 minutes
Apricots	4 minutes
Figs, pears, prunes	10 minutes
Peaches	5 minutes
Mixed fruit	10 minutes

Steamed puddings

Container
Use a heat resistant container, such as metal, boilable plastic, or ovenproof glass or china. Ensure that it is not too deep for

your pressure cooker. Allow a gap of at least 5cm/2 in between the top of the basin and the lid to allow steam to circulate.

Timing
The cooking times given in the table below are for puddings in metal or boilable plastic. When using ovenproof glass or china, add 10 minutes.

Basic method
1. Grease the container and fill no more than three-quarters to allow room for the pudding to rise.

2. Cover the container with greased foil or a double thickness of greased greaseproof paper, tying it down securely.

3. Stand the container on the trivet in the pressure cooker and pour in the recommended amount of boiling water.

4. Fit the lid and heat until a thin jet of steam escapes from the vent in the lid. Reduce the heat so that the pudding steams gently, without reaching HIGH pressure, for the recommended time, without the water boiling away furiously. It is during this steaming stage that the raising agent in the flour activates and the pudding rises.

5. At the end of the steaming time, bring to LOW pressure and cook for the time recommended in the table.

6. Reduce the pressure slowly at room temperature to prevent the pudding from sinking. Remove the pudding using oven gloves.

Increasing quantities
When increasing the quantities of a recipe, allow an extra 10 minutes' cooking time for every additional 55g/2 oz flour.

GUIDE TO ADAPTING STEAMED PUDDING RECIPES TO PRESSURE COOKING			
Normal Cooking Time	Water	Steaming	Pressure Cooking at LOW
30 minutes	850ml/1½ pints	5 minutes	10 minutes
1 hour	850ml/1½ pints	15 minutes	25 minutes
2-3 hours	1.2 litres/2 pints	20 minutes	1 hour

PRESERVES

A pressure cooker can be used for making jam, marmalade, conserves or curds, or for bottling fruit.

In jam making, pressure cooking speeds up the softening of the fruit and, since little liquid is added, the flavour is more concentrated and setting point is achieved more quickly.

A pressure cooker also offers a quicker and therefore cheaper alternative to oven bottling.

Jam making

The success of the jam depends on using good quality, undamaged fruit. Berry fruits such as raspberries and strawberries do not require softening under pressure but the open pressure cooker may be used as a large pan to prepare the jam in the traditional way.

1. The trivet is not used.

2. The softening stage releases the pectin from the fruit so that the jam will eventually set. Put the water and fruit into the pressure cooker, making sure that it is no more than half full. Fit the lid, bring to MEDIUM pressure and cook for up to 5 minutes, depending on the ripeness of the fruit and its type. Reduce the pressure slowly at room temperature.

3. Put the clean, dry jam-jars to warm in a low oven.

4. Calculate the amount of sugar required. This will be approximately equal to the weight of the fruit. Warm the sugar slightly in a bowl in a low oven as this helps it to dissolve quickly to give good colour and flavour.

5. Add the sugar and cook over a low heat, stirring continuously until dissolved. Do not fit the lid once the sugar has been added.

6. Bring to the boil and boil rapidly until the jam reaches setting point. You can gauge this most accurately with a sugar thermometer as setting occurs at 104°C/221°F. Alternatively, stir the jam with a wooden spoon, cool the spoon slightly and, if the jam partly gels, setting point has been reached. A third method is to remove the pressure cooker from the heat and spoon a little jam on to a cold saucer. Leave it to cool, then rub your finger over the surface – if it wrinkles, the jam is ready to set.

7. As soon as the jam reaches setting point, remove the pressure cooker from the heat.

8. Remove any scum. Stand the jars on newspaper (to help prevent them cracking) and ladle the jam into jars. (You may find it easier to ladle the jam into a heatproof jug first and then pour the jam into the jars rather than using a ladle.) Fill, cover with waxed discs and, when cool, cover and label.

Fruit bottling
Choose firm, unblemished fruit of equal size and ripeness to ensure even cooking. Fruit which discolours when peeled (such as apple), should be covered in a solution of 1 teaspoonful salt to 600ml/1 pint water until ready for bottling. Rinse well in cold water before packing the apple into the bottles.

Hard fruit (such as apples and pears) needs slight cooking before bottling. Put 300ml/½ pint water into the pressure cooker with the trivet and pile the fruit on the trivet, making sure that the pressure cooker is no more than half full. Fit the lid and bring to HIGH pressure. Reduce the pressure immediately in cold water to avoid overcooking.

As soft fruits (such as raspberries and strawberries) tend to shrink when cooked, it is best to soak them overnight in a heavy syrup before bottling.

Fruit bottled in a syrup will give better results in terms of flavour and colour but water can be used instead. When making the syrup, boil granulated sugar in water for about a minute. If you prefer a light syrup, use 55-115g/2-4 oz sugar for each 600ml/1 pint water. For a heavier syrup for desserts, use 175-225g/6-8 oz for each 600ml/1 pint water. When bottling fruit, use LOW pressure.

Method
1. Immerse the clean jars and lids in boiling water while preparing the fruit.

2. Pack the cleaned fruit into the jars. Pack tightly to the shoulder of the jar.

3. Bring the prepared syrup to the boil and, using a jug, pour into the jars, a little at a time, releasing any air bubbles by tapping the jar gently against a board. Leave a space at the top of about 5mm/¼ in.

4. Fit the rubber bands and tops. If the jars are sealed by metal clips, these should be fitted at this stage, but if metal screw bands are used, they should be screwed down until tight, then unscrewed for a quarter turn. This is to allow air and steam to escape from the jars during bottling. Return the jars to the hot water.

5. Put the trivet into the pressure cooker upside down and pour in 1.2 litres/2 pints boiling water. Stand the jars in the pressure cooker, making sure that they don't touch each other or the sides of the pressure cooker (otherwise they could crack).

6. Using a medium heat bring to LOW pressure and cook for the time recommended in the following table. Reduce pressure slowly at room temperature.

7. Remove the jars and screw tight the jars fitted with metal screw bands. Metal clips tighten automatically.

8. Test the seal the next day by unscrewing the bands or removing the clips. If the covers remain firmly in position, label the jars and store. If they can be removed, the fruit should be used as soon as possible and you should examine the bottle, cover, seal and band or clip as one of them could be faulty.

GUIDE TO BOTTLING FRUIT	
Fruit	**Time at LOW Pressure**
Apple, thickly sliced	1 minute
Apricots, halved and stoned	1 minute
Blackberries	1 minute
Cherries	1 minute
Damsons	1 minute
Gooseberries (only when firm)	1 minute
Greengages	1 minute
Loganberries	3 minutes
Peaches, skinned and halved	1 minute
Pears, halved or quartered	3 minutes
Pineapple, cubed	3 minutes
Plums, whole or halved	1 minute
Raspberries	1 minute
Rhubarb	2 minutes
Strawberries	3 minutes

32

Recipes

The following recipes were tested using the following pressures:

HIGH	15 lb
MEDIUM	10 lb
LOW	5 lb

If your pressure cooker operates at pressures different from these, here are some tips:

❖ Check with a similar recipe in your manufacturer's instruction/recipe book and use the cooking time as a guide.

❖ When a recipe that follows cooks at HIGH pressure and you need to use a lower pressure (say 12 lb), add a quarter to a third of the recommended cooking time, using the ingredient with the longest cooking time as a guide.

❖ When a recipe cooks at HIGH pressure and you need to use a lower pressure (say 7½ lb), double the cooking time, using the ingredient with the longest cooking time as a guide.

❖ When a recipe cooks at MEDIUM and you need to use a higher pressure (say 12 lb), reduce the cooking time by a few minutes, using the ingredient with the longest cooking time as a guide.

❖   When a recipe cooks at LOW and you need to use a
     higher pressure (say 6 lb or 7½ lb), reduce the cooking
     time slightly, using the ingredient with the longest cook-
     ing time as a guide.

STOCK

Makes about 600ml/1 pint   *40 minutes at HIGH pressure*

This stock will be more or less concentrated, depending on the quantity of bones used. As with soups generally, it is easier to dilute after cooking rather than make too weak a stock to start with.

bones or poultry carcass (cooked or raw)
2 carrots, scrubbed and sliced
1 onion, roughly chopped
6 peppercorns
bouquet garni
1 tsp salt

1. Put the bones or carcass into the pressure cooker and pour over 1 litre/1¾ pints water. Bring slowly to the boil in the open pan and, with a spoon, remove the scum from the surface.

2. Add the remaining ingredients.

3. Fit the lid, bring to HIGH pressure and cook for 40 minutes.

4. Reduce the pressure slowly at room temperature.

5. Cool slightly, strain into a container and, when cold, remove the fat from the top.

6. Chill until needed – up to 3-4 days – or freeze.

FISH STOCK

15 minutes at HIGH pressure

There's nothing quite like the delicate flavour of a homemade fish stock. Chill and use it the same day or freeze it for future use.

1 fish head and trimmings
1 onion, chopped
1 celery stick, sliced
6 peppercorns
a few parsley sprigs
bouquet garni
1 tsp salt

1. Wash the fish head and trimmings and put into the pressure cooker with the remaining ingredients. Pour over 1 litre/1¾ pints water.

2. Fit the lid, bring to HIGH pressure and cook for 15 minutes.

3. Reduce the pressure slowly at room temperature.

4. Strain the stock. It's now ready to use.

MIXED VEGETABLE SOUP

Serves 4-6   *10 minutes at HIGH pressure*

Served with crusty bread, this could be a main course soup. Vary your choice of vegetables according to the seasons.

25g/1 oz butter
2 medium onions, finely chopped
4 large carrots, cut into 1cm/½ in slices
2 large parsnips, cut into 1cm/½ in slices
4 large potatoes, cut into 1cm/½ in slices
2 medium leeks, thinly sliced
1 litre/1¾ pints chicken, beef or vegetable stock
salt and freshly ground black pepper
dash of Worcestershire sauce
freshly grated Cheddar cheese, to serve (optional)

1. Melt the butter in the open pressure cooker and gently cook the onions, stirring occasionally, until softened but not browned.

2. Add the remaining ingredients.

3. Fit the lid, bring to HIGH pressure and cook for 10 minutes.

4. Reduce the pressure slowly at room temperature. Adjust the seasoning to taste and serve just as it is or topped with grated cheese.

COCK-A-LEEKIE SOUP

Serves 4   *7 minutes at HIGH pressure*

This soup, based on the traditional Scottish version, takes only minutes in the pressure cooker.

4 skinless chicken thighs
1 litre/1¾ pints chicken stock
1 medium onion, finely chopped
4 medium leeks, cut into 2.5cm/1 in slices
4 ready-to-eat prunes, stones removed
salt and freshly ground black pepper
1 tbsp lemon juice

1. Put the chicken into the pressure cooker with the stock. Bring to the boil and, with a spoon, skim the surface.

2. Stir in the remaining ingredients.

3. Fit the lid, bring to HIGH pressure and cook for 7 minutes.

4. Reduce the pressure slowly at room temperature.

5. Lift out the chicken, cut the meat off the bones and chop into small pieces. Discard the bones.

6. Return the chopped chicken to the soup, adjust the seasoning to taste and reheat before serving.

BEEF WITH VEGETABLES

Serves 4   *15 minutes at* HIGH *pressure*

Use this recipe as the basis for a delicious stew; vary the meat and vegetables according to personal preference and seasonal availability.

675g/1½ lb lean stewing steak, cut into cubes
25g/1 oz flour
2 tbsp oil
2 medium onions, chopped
225g/8 oz carrots, sliced
450g/1 lb potatoes, thickly sliced
2 medium parsnips, sliced
2 medium leeks, sliced
600ml/1 pint beef or vegetable stock
salt and freshly ground black pepper
1 bay leaf
1 tbsp fresh chopped parsley, for garnish

1. Toss the steak in the flour (easy in a freezer bag).

2. Heat the oil in the open pressure cooker, add the onions and cook, stirring occasionally, until softened but not browned.

3. Add the steak and cook, stirring occasionally, until browned.

4. Add the remaining ingredients except the parsley. Fit the lid, bring to HIGH pressure and cook for 15 minutes. Reduce the pressure quickly in cold water.

5. Remove the bay leaf, adjust the seasoning to taste and serve garnished with parsley.

COD PROVENÇALE

This is good served with thick slices of toasted French bread.

1 tbsp olive oil
1 medium onion, finely chopped
1 garlic clove, crushed
675g/1½ lb thick cod fillet, cut into 4 portions
400g can chopped tomatoes
1 green pepper, seeds removed and chopped
1 tbsp tomato purée
½ tsp brown sugar
1 bay leaf
salt and freshly ground black pepper
1 tbsp chopped fresh parsley

1.   Heat the oil in the open pressure cooker, add the onion and cook, stirring occasionally, until softened but not browned.

2.   Add the remaining ingredients, except the parsley.

3.   Fit the lid, bring to HIGH pressure and cook for 4 minutes.

4.   Reduce the pressure quickly with cold water.

5.   Remove the bay leaf before serving and sprinkle with parsley.

CABBAGE IN A CREAMY SAUCE

Serves 4   *4 minutes at HIGH pressure*

This is particularly good served with boiled ham or with grilled thick sausages.

25g/1 oz butter
1 medium onion, finely chopped
1 small or ½ a large white cabbage, finely shredded
150ml/¼ pint chicken stock
salt and freshly ground black pepper
good pinch of grated nutmeg
1 tbsp cornflour
150ml/¼ pint milk

1. Melt the butter in the open pressure cooker, add the onion and cook gently, stirring occasionally, until softened but not browned.

2. Add the cabbage, stock and seasoning, mixing well.

3. Fit the lid, bring to HIGH pressure and cook for 4 minutes.

4. Reduce the pressure quickly in cold water.

5. Blend the cornflour with the milk to make a smooth cream. Stir into the cabbage and bring to the boil, stirring continuously, until thickened.

EGG CUSTARD

Serves 4   *10 minutes at* HIGH *pressure*

This is such an easy dessert to make, and best served chilled with fresh or cooked fruit.

butter
425ml/¾ pint milk
3 medium eggs
55g/2 oz caster sugar
½ tsp vanilla extract
freshly ground nutmeg

1. Grease a 600ml/1 pint pudding basin or soufflé dish with some butter.

2. In a saucepan, gently heat the milk until warm but not hot.

3. In a bowl, lightly whisk the eggs with the sugar and vanilla.

4. Add the warm milk to the egg mixture and stir well.

5. Pour the custard mixture into the prepared dish. Sprinkle with a little nutmeg and cover securely with grease-proof paper or foil.

6. Put the trivet into the pressure cooker and stand the dish on top. Pour in 300ml/½ pint boiling water.

7. Fit the lid, bring to HIGH pressure and cook for 10 minutes until set.

8. Reduce the pressure slowly at room temperature.

9. Carefully lift the dish from the pressure cooker, leave to cool then chill.

APPLES WITH HONEYED FRUIT

Serves 4   *4-6 minutes at HIGH pressure*

butter
4 cooking apples, washed and cored
140g/5 oz mixed dried fruit, such as sultanas and chopped apricots and cherries
2 tbsp honey
2 tbsp soft brown sugar

1.   Grease four squares of foil with some butter and stand an apple in the centre of each.

2.   Mix together the remaining ingredients and spoon into the apple centres (any left over can be put to the side of the apples). Crimp the foil at the edges to form a saucer shape.

3.   Put the trivet into the pressure cooker with 300ml/ ½ pint water. Stand the apples and saucers on the trivet, ensuring that the apples do not touch the sides of the pressure cooker.

4.   Fit the lid, bring to HIGH pressure and cook for 4-6 minutes.

5.   Reduce the pressure quickly in cold water.

6.   Lift out the apples on their saucers and transfer to serving dishes, discarding the foil.

Tip: For a change, add almond extract or ground mixed spice to the filling mixture in step 2.

PEARS IN RED WINE

Serves 4   *8 minutes at HIGH pressure*

Serve just as they are or with a dollop of thick cream or crème fraîche. The cooking time will depend on the ripeness of the pears.

4 large firm pears
300ml/½ pint red wine
55g/2 oz caster sugar
¼ tsp ground cinnamon
strip of lemon peel

1. Peel the pears, leaving the stalks intact. Shave a thin slice off the bottom of each pear so that it will stand upright.

2. Pour the wine into the pressure cooker, without the trivet, and add the sugar, cinnamon and lemon peel.

3. Heat gently, stirring continuously, until the sugar has dissolved.

4. Stand the pears upright in the pressure cooker, ensuring that they do not touch the sides. Spoon the liquid over the pears.

5. Fit the lid, bring to HIGH pressure, and cook for about 8 minutes until the pears are soft.

6. Reduce the pressure quickly in cold water.

7. Using a spoon, lift the pears into a serving dish (don't be tempted to lift them by the stalks – they could break off). Pour the wine mixture over the pears.

8. Cool completely and chill before serving.

FILLED PEACHES WITH ALMONDS

Serves 4   *3 minutes at HIGH pressure*

4 large firm peaches
25g/1 oz brown sugar
25g/1 oz soft butter
1 medium egg yolk
55g/2 oz digestive biscuits, crumbled
25g/1 oz chopped toasted almonds
25g/1 oz caster sugar
300ml/½ pint dry white wine
toasted flaked almonds, to serve

1. Peel the peaches (cover with boiling water, leave to stand for 5 minutes and they should peel easily). Halve and remove the stones.

2. Combine the brown sugar and butter until well blended. Beat in the egg yolk and stir in the biscuit crumbs and chopped toasted almonds.

3. Spoon the mixture into the peach cavities.

4. Put the caster sugar and wine into the open pressure cooker, without the trivet, and heat gently until the sugar has dissolved. Stand the filled peach halves in the wine.

5. Fit the lid, bring to HIGH pressure and cook for 3 minutes.

6. Reduce the pressure quickly in cold water.

7. Leave to cool and then chill until required. Serve sprinkled with toasted flaked almonds.

Tip: Serve with cream or yoghurt drizzled over the top.

Fan Ovens

33

Cooking with a Fan Oven

Cooking is a natural process. As the air in the oven is heated it produces convection currents. The hotter air rises to the top whilst the cooler air can be found at the bottom of the oven. As the heat penetrates the food, the outside browns and the inside cooks and so becomes edible and suitable for the human digestive system. Depending on the type of food and temperature used, the process may be short or long.

Conventional ovens use this natural process and, to get the best results, instructions are given which indicate the specific shelf position to use. Older recipe instructions may simply give guidance; for example, they may merely suggest using the top, middle or bottom of the oven.

Fan ovens, technically known as 'forced air convection ovens', use the same natural principle but by placing a fan inside the oven the air is moved more quickly and evenly around it. The fan is usually situated in the vicinity of the heating source and will circulate the heat from either the sides or the back of the oven.

Although the noise of the fan may sound as if the air is being blasted around the oven, the movement of air is actually very gentle.

By inserting a fan into the oven, the cook gets many benefits of which you need to be aware. Manufacturers often supply a recipe book, which should be followed, but problems sometimes arise when you want to use a recipe originally created for cooking in a conventional oven.

34

Using Conventional Recipes in a Fan Oven

Shelf positions – don't worry
As the air in a fan oven is evenly distributed, there is no need to worry about which shelf position to use. An additional bonus is that all the shelves can be used at the same time. This is very useful when cooking bulk quantities, perhaps for the freezer or for an event where a large quantity of food is needed.

Cooking from cold – it can be done
With the aid of a fan, the oven heats up more quickly than a conventional oven so preheating is of lesser importance. Even so, some recipes, particularly cakes and pastries, are cooked better by preheating first. Should you decide to cook from cold you may need to add about 5-10 minutes to the overall cooking time. Unless the cooker manufacturer gives specific instructions to cook from frozen, food must be thawed before cooking.

Oven temperatures – are different
When cooking in a fan oven, the internal oven temperatures may be 10-20 degrees lower than those used in a conventional oven. To use a favourite conventional recipe, check in the manufacturer's recipe book or check the chart given on page 257 for guidance.

Cooking times – are faster
As the oven heats up so quickly, the cooking operation becomes faster so, when using your own recipes, reduce the cooking time by about 10 minutes for every hour of cooking.

Saving energy – no effort required
You do nothing, simply enjoy the fact that the oven is cooking more quickly and, if you wish, you can cook more at the same time. The amount of energy used will be less, which means money is also saved.

35

Oven Temperature
Conversion Chart

Opposite is the oven temperature conversion chart. Select the conventional temperature from the appropriate column (given in *italics*), then match it with the suggested fan oven temperature for your particular model (given in **bold**).

The oven thermostat
While the oven is heating, an indicator light will be 'on'. When the oven has reached the temperature selected on the oven control dial, the light will go 'out'.

During the cooking period, the light will come 'on' and go 'out' at intervals. This shows that the oven temperature is being maintained.

GAS MARK	FAN OVEN ELECTRIC °C	CONVENTIONAL ELECTRIC OVEN °C	CONVENTIONAL ELECTRIC OVEN °F
¼	100°	100°	200°
¼	110°	110°	225°
½	115°	130°	250°
1	125°	140°	275°
2	135°	150°	300°
3	145°	160°	325°
4-5	165/175°	180/190°	350/375°
6	185°	200°	400°
7	205°	220°	425°
8	215°	230°	450°
9	235°	250°	475°

(Reproduced with thanks to NEFF.)

Important
The conversion chart is for guidance only. Slight variations can be expected.

36

Using the Oven

Each oven has its own characteristics and, once you are familiar with them, you will be aware of any slight adjustments you may need to make to suit your recipes. If you don't select the exact correct temperature on the control dial each time you use it, the thermostat will, of course, operate slightly differently. If the kitchen is very hot or cold, this will affect the heating up time.

When preheating: the oven is preheated when the indicator light goes 'out'.

The heat distribution of the oven has been engineered to give the best possible circulation. Never line shelves or cover the oven interior with foil as the oven will not perform correctly.

Before heating the oven, remove any oven furniture that is not required – that includes oven shelves and baking trays or dishes. Why waste time and electricity heating things which are not needed?

The fan oven has been sold since the late sixties and there are still many old models in use today. The latest ovens are so fast that preheating takes only a few minutes and, as a result, most do not need to be preheated. Check your manufacturer's handbook for instructions about your particular model.

Roasting tips
❖ Always ensure that meat, poultry and game are completely thawed before cooking. This ensures a better-cooked result and reduces splashing in the oven.

258

❖ To reduce splashing and smoking during cooking, use a large meat tin for very large joints and birds and a smaller one for smaller quantities.

❖ Roasting bags and foil can be used but follow the manufacturer's instructions if you want to achieve the best result.

❖ Many years ago water used to be added to the roasting tin. With modern ovens this is unnecessary.

❖ Some meat is tough. To tenderise it, marinate it for several hours before cooking. You can either rub the meat with the marinade or immerse it. A basic marinade is two tablespoonfuls of oil to one tablespoonful of vinegar or lemon juice.

❖ Joints and poultry can be carved more easily if left to stand for 10-15 minutes after cooking.

❖ When roasting large joints of meat or poultry, the oven can be turned off about 10 minutes before the end of the cooking time to save even more energy.

❖ Stuffing poultry is not advised as there could be a chance that the meat around the stuffing is not sufficiently cooked. Should you feel that you want to use a stuffing, then stuff the neck end where there is sufficient loose skin to contain it.

Baking tips

❖ Cakes are best made in a warm kitchen; the room temperature should not be below 17-20°C/65-70°F.

❖ All the ingredients should be at room temperature unless it is fat being used for a rubbing in mixture when it should be used straight from the refrigerator.

❖ Most recipes for cakes and pastries are best cooked after the oven is preheated.

❖ Use the tin and container sizes given in a recipe. If you have to use a different size, be prepared for a slightly different cooking time and possibly a different result.

❖ Self-raising flours and raising agents such as baking powder, bicarbonate of soda and cream of tartar should be as fresh as possible as they lose their strength with overlong storage.

Preparation of cake tins

Where a recipe calls for a tin to be greased and lined, lightly grease the inside of the tin with butter or margarine and then line with greaseproof paper. To do this, cut out a circle to fit the base of the tin and then a long strip to cover the total circumference of the tin. This strip lining should be about 5cm/2 in higher than the depth of the tin. Place the strip on a flat surface and make a horizontal fold of about 2.5cm/1 in. Using scissors, cut diagonally at about 2.5cm/1 in intervals up to the point where the paper is folded. Arrange the lining around the inside of the tin and then place the circle of paper on the base.

To grease and flour a tin

Grease the inside with butter or margarine and sprinkle about a teaspoonful of flour over the base. Then, tap the sides of the tin, both while holding the tin level and while moving it slightly up and down, to coat all the inside surfaces evenly. Tip the tin upside down and tap on a hard surface to get rid of any excess flour.

Measurements of ingredients

Although metric measurements are officially in use, you may prefer to use imperial measures. For your convenience both are quoted. However, as the conversions have been altered to make weighing easier, it is important to remember only to use one and not to skip from one to the other in any one recipe, otherwise the recipe will not be successful.

37

Recipes

SPICY HADDOCK

Serves 4   *Preparation and cooking time: 1¼-1½ hours*

2 tbsp vegetable oil
1 small onion, peeled and chopped
1 clove garlic, crushed
2 tbsp soy sauce
1 level tsp dried mixed herbs
½ tsp curry powder
260g/9 oz can tomatoes, chopped with juice
50g/2 oz button mushrooms, sliced
salt and pepper
550g/1¼ lb haddock fillet, skinned and cut into pieces

1. Heat the oil in a pan and gently cook the onion and garlic until the onion is soft.

2. Stir in the soy sauce, herbs, curry powder, tomatoes and juice and mushrooms. Season to taste.

3. Place the fish into a buttered 1 litre/2 pint casserole dish, pour over the sauce, cover and cook from cold at 150°C for 60-70 minutes or until the fish is cooked. (If using a pre-heated oven you may need to reduce the cooking time by about 5-10 minutes.)

FOIL-BAKED SALMON

Serves 8-12 depending on the size of the salmon

Preparation time: 15 minutes

Cooking time: allow 24 minutes per kg or 12 minutes per lb

1 whole salmon, cleaned and gutted
butter or margarine
salt and pepper
1 lemon, cut into slices
bunch of parsley
juice of 1 lemon

1. Tear off a piece of foil twice the size of the salmon and grease thoroughly with butter.

2. Season the salmon inside and out, and place on the foil.

3. Place the lemon slices and the parsley inside the body cavity. Pour the lemon juice over the salmon.

4. Enclose the salmon in the foil, tightly sealing the edges.

5. Place in a roasting pan and cook from cold at 160°C, allowing 24 minutes per kg or 12 minutes per lb. (If using a preheated oven, you may need to reduce the cooking time by about 5-10 minutes.)

PILCHARD AND TOMATO LOAF

Serves 4   *Preparation and cooking time: 1¼-1½ hours*

This makes an inexpensive nutritious meal, which can be served hot or cold. It is also a useful recipe for picnics or lunch boxes.

15g/½ oz butter or margarine, melted
424g/16 oz can pilchards, drained
400g/15 oz can chopped tomatoes
1 small onion, peeled and finely chopped
50g/2 oz fresh brown breadcrumbs
2 level tsp dried mixed herbs
2 medium eggs, lightly beaten
salt and pepper

1.   Line a 650g/1½ lb loaf tin with foil and brush with the butter.

2.   In a bowl, mix together the pilchards, tomatoes, onion, breadcrumbs, herbs and eggs. Season to taste. Transfer to the loaf tin and smooth over the top.

3.   Cook from cold at 180°C for 45-50 minutes. (If using a preheated oven, you may need to reduce the cooking time by about 5-10 minutes.) Allow to cool before turning out onto a serving dish.

SAUSAGE, ONION AND TOMATO CASSEROLE

Serves 4   *Preparation and cooking time: 1½-1¾ hours*

If preferred, the tomatoes can be substituted with stock.

2 tbsp vegetable oil
1 large onion, peeled and sliced
8 thick sausages, chopped in half
400g/14 oz can chopped tomatoes with herbs
1 beef stock cube, crumbled
2 tbsp tomato sauce
salt and pepper

1. Heat the oil in a pan and gently fry the onion until soft. Remove the onion and add the sausages. Fry until browned on all sides.

2. Add the onion, tomatoes, beef stock cube, tomato sauce and salt and pepper to taste. Bring to the boil, cover and simmer for 5-10 minutes.

3. Pour into a 1.2 litre/2 pint casserole dish, cover and cook in a preheated oven at 150°C for 1-1¼ hours or until the sausages are cooked through.

LAMB HOTPOT

Serves 4   *Preparation and cooking time: 1¾-2¼ hours*

4 lamb chops with a total weight of 500g/1 lb 2 oz
2 large onions, peeled and sliced
2 carrots, peeled and sliced
2 large potatoes, peeled and sliced
salt and pepper
500ml/1 pint hot meat or vegetable stock
vegetable oil for brushing

1. In a 2 litre/4 pint casserole dish, layer the chops, vegetables and salt and pepper to taste. Finish with a top layer of potatoes.

2. Pour over the hot stock and brush the potato topping with oil.

3. Cover the casserole with the lid and cook in a preheated oven at 150°C for 1¾-2 hours or until the meat is tender. (This recipe can be cooked from cold but you may need to add about 5-10 minutes to the cooking time.)

Tip: As an alternative, try using pork chops instead of lamb.

TURKEY LOAF

Serves 4-6   *Preparation and cooking time: 1-1½ hours*

This is a good recipe for using up left over turkey or chicken, especially around the festive season. It can be eaten hot or cold and served with vegetables, salad or crispy bread.

7 streaky bacon rashers, rinds removed
25g/1 oz butter or margarine
1 medium onion, peeled and finely chopped
75g/3 oz fresh white breadcrumbs
1 level tsp dried tarragon
350g/12 oz cooked turkey, finely chopped
140ml/¼ pint chicken stock
2 medium eggs, lightly beaten
salt and pepper

1. Stretch the rashers of bacon with the back of a knife and line the base and sides of a 15cm/6 in soufflé dish with the bacon.

2. Melt the butter in a pan and lightly fry the onion.

3. Place the breadcrumbs in a bowl and stir in the onion and butter, tarragon, turkey, stock and eggs. Season to taste.

4. Pour the mixture into the bacon-lined dish and bake in a preheated oven at 160°C for 45-60 minutes.

PORK IN CIDER

Serves 4   *Preparation and cooking time: 1¾-2 hours*

Although less usual, veal could be used instead of pork.

50g/2 oz butter or margarine
2 tsp vegetable oil
1 medium onion, peeled and chopped
½ red pepper, deseeded and diced
1 stick celery, finely chopped
550g/1¼ lb pork, diced
25g/1 oz plain flour, seasoned with salt and pepper
285ml/½ pint strong dry cider
140ml/¼ pint chicken stock
1 level tsp dried marjoram
salt and pepper
1 dessert apple, washed, cored and cut into thick slices

1. Melt the butter and oil in a pan. Stir in the onion, pepper and celery. Gently cook the vegetables until softened.

2. Toss the meat in the flour and stir into the vegetables. Cook until sealed and lightly browned.

3. Gradually add the cider and stock and bring to the boil. Add the marjoram and season to taste. Boil for about 2 minutes.

4. Arrange the apple in the base of a casserole dish and spoon the pork mixture over. Cover and cook in a preheated oven at 160°C for 1¼-1½ hours or until the pork is tender.

GLAZED GAMMON

Serves 4   *Preparation time: 15 minutes*

Cooking time: allow 30 minutes per 450g/1 lb and 30 minutes extra

1 gammon joint

GLAZE
1 tbsp thick cut marmalade
15g/½ oz melted butter
1 tsp dried mustard

1. Wrap the joint with foil and place into a roasting tin.

2. Roast in a preheated oven at 170°C for 30 minutes per 450g/lb and 30 minutes extra.

3. Mix together the marmalade, butter and mustard.

4. Remove the gammon skin 30 minutes before the end of cooking and brush the glaze over the fat. Return to the oven to complete the cooking time.

Tip: This recipe can be cooked from cold but you may need to add about 5-10 minutes to the cooking time.

STUFFED MARROW

Serves 4   *Preparation and cooking time: 1¾-2 hours*

1 onion, peeled and finely chopped
2 tomatoes, skinned and chopped
65g/2½ oz fresh white or brown breadcrumbs
350g/12 oz minced beef
1 tbsp tomato sauce
1 level tsp dried mixed herbs
salt and pepper
900g/2 lb marrow, washed, cut into four rings and seeds
  removed

1.   Mix together the onion, tomatoes, breadcrumbs, beef,
      tomato sauce, herbs and salt and pepper to taste. Spoon
      the mixture into the marrow rings.

2.   Place in a greased baking tin measuring 17.5 x 22.5cm/
      7 x 9 in. Cover and bake in a pre-heated oven at 160°C
      for 1½-1¾ hours. Remove the cover for the last 15
      minutes of cooking. Avoid overcooking as the marrow
      contains a lot of water and may collapse.

3.   Serve with a white cheese sauce, if desired.

Tip: This recipe can be cooked from cold but you may need to
add about 5-10 minutes to the cooking time.

QUEEN OF PUDDINGS

Serves 4-5   *Preparation and cooking time: 1¼-1½ hours*

550ml/1 pint milk
2 level tsp caster sugar
½ tsp lemon essence
75g/3 oz fresh white breadcrumbs
2 medium egg yolks

TOPPING
2-3 tbsp jam
2 medium egg whites
50g/2 oz caster sugar
caster sugar for dredging

1. In a pan, warm the milk and stir in the sugar and essence. Place the breadcrumbs in a bowl and pour over the milk. Leave to stand for 30 minutes.

2. Stir in the egg yolks and pour the mixture into a buttered 1.2 litre/2 pint pie dish. Bake in a pre-heated oven at 160°C for 35-40 minutes or until the mixture is set and the top has formed a skin. Remove from the oven.

3. Warm the jam in a pan. In a separate bowl, whisk the egg whites until stiff and fold in the sugar.

4. Drizzle the jam over the pudding and then gently spread the meringue over the top. Sprinkle with sugar and return to the oven for 6-8 minutes or until the meringue is browned.

BANANA LOAF

Makes 8 slices   *Preparation and cooking time: 2-2½ hours*

100g/4 oz butter or margarine
150g/6 oz caster sugar
2 medium eggs
450g/1 lb bananas, peeled and mashed
few drops of banana essence, optional
225g/8 oz self raising flour

1. In a bowl, cream the butter and sugar until light and fluffy. Beat in the eggs one at a time.

2. Beat in the banana with the essence.

3. Sieve the flour and fold into the banana mixture.

4. Line a greased 900g/2 lb loaf tin with greaseproof paper. Spoon in the mixture and smooth it.

5. Bake in a preheated oven at 150°C for 1-1¼ hours or until golden brown and when a small pointed knife inserted into the centre of the cake comes out clean.

6. Remove and leave in the tin for 5 minutes. Loosen the sides and turn out onto a wire cooling tray. Remove the greaseproof paper and leave to stand until cold.

MELTING MOMENTS

Makes 20 biscuits

Preparation and cooking time: 25-35 minutes

These are some of my really favourite biscuits. I used to cook them at school and they never reached my home!

100g/4 oz butter
100g/4 oz caster sugar
1 medium egg
few drops of vanilla essence
150g/6 oz self raising flour
pinch salt
40g/1½ oz rolled oats

1. In a bowl, cream the butter and sugar together until light and fluffy. Beat in the egg and essence.

2. In another bowl, sieve the flour with the salt and stir into the butter mixture.

3. With wet hands, divide the mixture into 20 pieces and form each piece into a ball.

4. Roll each ball in the oats and place onto greased baking trays, allowing room for the biscuits to spread. Bake in a preheated oven at 190°C for 15-20 minutes.

5. Remove, and leave on the trays for 3-4 minutes before transferring them, using a palette knife, onto a wire cooling tray.

Freezing

38

The Freezer

Freezing involves reducing the temperature of food to a level when chemical changes are slowed down and micro-organisms are inactivated. Food is frozen to (and maintained at) a temperature of -18°C/0°F or lower to keep the food in the same condition as when it first entered the freezer. When the food is thawed or defrosted, deterioration begins again. For this reason food which has been defrosted should not be refrozen. Raw food should always be cooked before refreezing and defrosted cooked food should always be used at once (to avoid the possibility of food poisoning).

Freezing must be completed speedily. If food is frozen slowly, unduly large ice crystals are formed within the food. Foods with a high moisture content are the most affected. As the crystals expand during freezing they puncture the food cells. The cells then collapse during thawing, producing a poor (often discoloured) result.

The faster food is frozen, the better its original condition is maintained. Fast freezing is usually controlled by a fast-freeze switch. When switched on it overrides the thermostat causing the temperature to fall. It continues to fall as new food freezes. Meanwhile, neither the temperature of the cabinet, nor the temperature of the frozen food already in the freezer, rises. Some freezers have a separate compartment for fast freezing instead, so that new, warmer food does not affect other areas. Follow your manufacturer's instructions for freezing food if you are to obtain best results when defrosting, reheating or cooking.

Star ratings

One large white and three small dark stars on a freezer means it can freeze fresh food at a lower temperature than -18°C/0°F, which is ideal for storing. Freezing areas in fridges have ratings which correspond to symbols on pre-packed frozen foods:

STAR RATING	TEMPERATURE	STORAGE TIME
Three stars	−18°C/0°F	Three months
Two stars	−12°C/10°F	One month
One star	−6°C/21°F	One week

Whether you choose a chest or an upright freezer will depend mainly on where you intend to position it. A chest freezer is more economical to run, with more storage space, but it takes up a lot of floor space. An upright freezer or fridge/freezer is usually more suitable for the kitchen.

39

Checkpoints for Freezing

❖ Use containers, dishes and plates suitable both for freezer *and* your most likely cooking method – be that oven, hob or microwave. This way home-made food may be frozen, defrosted and then perhaps even heated or cooked in the same container. Wrap and seal the container securely, using freezer foil or a heavy duty freezer bag. If you wish to use the container while the food is in the freezer, line the dish with foil, pour in the food, freeze it, remove the food and wrap and label it before returning it to your freezer. To defrost; remove the wrapping, return the frozen block to its container, cover and defrost.

❖ Cook extra portions of food, whatever method you choose to cook by. Freeze them so that meals and snacks can be defrosted and then reheated easily.

❖ Freeze single portions – especially helpful for microwave use: an individual meal can then be ready in minutes without any food preparation. For the same reason, freeze small items (e.g. sausages, bacon rashers, chops, etc.) individually. They can then be packed and sealed in one large parcel but defrosted in whatever quantity may be required later. Some foods can be cut into individual portions prior to freezing – such as pies, pizzas, savoury and sweet flans, cakes. No need to defrost the whole dish, some of which might be wasted as a consequence.

❖ Cool all foods completely before freezing and freeze covered (particularly plated meals destined for reheating in the microwave).

40

The Microwave/Freezer Friendship

Whilst it is true that any form of cooking can be used when preparing food for the freezer, it can be argued that a microwave oven is a perfect companion to a freezer and vice versa. The freezer no longer remains just another storage area but can become part of your system of cooking. At first, some extra thought will need to be given to the use of the two appliances in conjunction, but in a short time you will have perfected it to suit your own needs. Do not be put off by mistakes – learn from them and successes will soon outweigh failures.

Our grandmothers had baking days, making a week's supply of bread and cakes. Fruit and vegetables were bottled for the winter months. Laborious hours were spent in the kitchen. Today, freezer owners are able to take advantage of their own garden produce, cheap seasonal foods and bulk buys. Additionally, we all agree that saving time can mean saving money. Food stored in the freezer is ready for immediate use with the speedy defrosting, cooking and/or reheating in the microwave oven. The freezer (particularly if it is well-stocked) and the microwave are economical to run too. The speedy cooking of the microwave can mean marked savings on fuel bills.

Just as freezing is one of the easiest and safest methods of preservation, so is microwaving one of the easiest and safest methods of cooking. Both appliances help produce meals containing foods which have retained the maximum natural colour, quality and flavour. Used in conjunction with other kitchen equipment, e.g. hob, conventional oven, grill and so on, the combinations with which to produce mouth-watering meals, with a minimum of time 'slaving' in the kitchen, are endless.

Frozen food no longer takes hours to defrost. It can take minutes only, so there is no need to plan meals hours in advance of eating, and you can take meals in your stride when unexpected visitors arrive at the door – hungry.

However, the microwave energy with which you can achieve this speedy defrosting must be applied with care. The smallest ice crystals melt first and, if frozen food is subjected to a continuous period of microwave energy, the areas which have melted first begin to heat up while adjacent parts remain frozen. The result is unsatisfactory with hot and frozen food in the same dish. Better results are obtained when the microwave energy is applied in short bursts with rests between. The periods of rest allow warmth from the defrosted food to be conducted to the frozen areas and ensure that the larger ice crystals also begin to melt. See the earlier microwave cooking section for more details about defrosting using a microwave cooker, particularly the AUTO-DEFROST setting.

Index

A

Aduki beans, microwaving, 62
Anchovy butter, 148
Apples, bottling, 235, 237
, microwaving, 63
, pressure cooking, 231, 232
, slow cooking, 191
, steaming, 97
with Honeyed Fruit, 248
Apricots, bottling, 237
, pressure cooking, 231, 232
, steaming, 97
, Tipsy, 200
Artichokes, blanching, 228
, pressure cooking, 225
, steaming, 91
Asparagus, blanching, 228
, pressure cooking, 225
, steaming, 91
Aubergines, processing, 142

B

Baby food, blending, 119
Bacon, defrosting, 56
, microwaving, 58
, pressure cooking, 220
Baking fish, 187
Banana Loaf, 271
Bananas, steaming, 97

Bass, pressure cooking, 223
, steaming, 95
Beans, blanching, 228
, dried, 62, 177-178, 206, 227
, microwaving, 62
, pressure cooking, 206, 225,
227
, slow cooking, 177-178
, steaming, 91
Beef, defrosting, 56
, microwaving, 58
, pressure cooking, 220
, slow cooking, 186
with Ginger and Spring
Onions, 72
with Vegetables, 244
Beetroot, blanching, 228
, pressure cooking, 225
, processing, 142
Soup with Soured Cream
and Dill, 122
Berry fruits, slow cooking, 191
Biscuits, blending, 119
, processing, 148
Black-eye beans, microwaving,
62
Blackberries, bottling, 237
, pressure cooking, 231
Blackcurrants, microwaving, 63
, pressure cooking, 231

, processing, 144
Blanching vegetables, 228
Borlotti, pressure cooking, 227
Bottling fruit, 235-237
Bread, processing, 146-147
Breadcrumbs, making, 118, 148
Bream, pressure cooking, 223
Brill, pressure cooking, 223
Brisket in a Pot, 193
Broccoli, blanching, 228
    , pressure cooking, 226
    Soup, 192
    , steaming, 91
Brussels sprouts, blanching, 228
    , pressure cooking, 226
    , steaming, 91
Bulgar wheat, steaming, 94
    with Herbs and Lemon, 101
Butter beans, pressure cooking,
    227
        , processing, 148

C
Cabbage in a Creamy Sauce,
    246
    , pressure cooking, 226
    , processing, 142
    , steaming, 92
Cake tins, preparing, 260
Cakes, baking in a fan oven,
    259-260
    , microwaving, 65-66
    , processing, 147
    , slow cooking, 191
Cannellini beans, microwaving,
    62
Carrots, blanching, 228
    , pressure cooking, 226
    , slow cooking, 188, 189
    , steaming, 92
Casserole, Chicken and
    Mushroom, 195
    , Fish and Butter Bean, 71
    of Lamb, Spicy, 157
    , Sausage, Onion and
        Tomato, 266
Casseroles, reheating, 37

Casseroling fish, 187-188
    vegetables, 189
Cauliflower, blanching, 229
    , pressure cooking, 226
    Soup, Cream of, 153
    , steaming, 92
Celeriac, steaming, 92
Celery, blanching, 229
    , pressure cooking, 226
    , processing, 142
    , slow cooking, 188
Cheese, chopping with a
    blender, 118
    , grating, 148
    , microwaving, 59
    , processing, 148
    Sauce, 68
Cherries, bottling, 237
    , pressure cooking, 231
Chick peas, microwaving, 62
Chicken and Mushroom
    Casserole, 195
    , defrosting, 56
    in a Packet with Tarragon
        and Cream Sauce, 104
    Liver Pâté, 154
    , microwaving, 58
    , pressure cooking, 220
    , slow cooking, 186
    , steaming, 96
    , Sweet and Sour, 158
Chicory, blanching, 229
    , pressure cooking, 226
Chinese leaves, steaming, 92
Chocolate, chopping with a
    blender, 118
    Mousse, White, 76
    , processing, 148
Chops, defrosting, 56
Christmas pudding, reheating,
    36
Clams, steaming, 95
Cock-a-Leekie Soup, 243
Cockles, steaming, 95
Coconut, chopping with a
    blender, 118
    Creams with Mango, 108

Cod, pressure cooking, 223
  Provençale, 245
  , steaming, 95
Coffee beans, grinding, 119
Corn on the Cob with Onion
  and Herb Butter, 99
  , steaming, 92
Courgettes, blanching, 229
  , pressure cooking, 226
  , processing, 142
  , slow cooking, 188
  , steaming, 92
Couscous, steaming, 94
Crab, pressure cooking, 223
Cream of Cauliflower Soup,
  153
  of Tomato Soup, 69
  , processing, 148-149
Creamed soups, 138-139
Cucumber, processing, 143
Curry, Vegetarian, 197
Custard, Egg, 247

D
Damsons, bottling, 237
  , pressure cooking, 231
Date and Walnut Pudding, 202
Defrosting, 32 *et seq.*
Dip, Fresh Herb, 121
Dips, processing, 140
Dried fruit, 149, 232
Drinks, reheating, 37
Duck, pressure cooking, 220
  , slow cooking, 186
  , steaming, 96

E
Egg Custard, 247
Eggs in Dishes with Cream and
  Herbs, 98
  , microwaving, 59
  , scrambled, 42
  , steaming, 90
  with Pancetta, 98

F
Fan oven:
  baking, 259
  preheating, 258
  roasting, 258-259
  temperature conversion chart,
    257
Fennel, processing, 143
Figs, pressure cooking, 232
Fish and Butter Bean Casserole,
  71
  , braising, 223
  , defrosting, 52, 87, 94, 216
  en papillote, 222
  , microwaving, 51 *et seq.*
  , pressure cooking, 221-223
  , slow cooking, 174, 186-188
  , steaming, 88, 94-96
  , stewing, 223
  with Summer Dressing, 70
Flageolet beans, microwaving,
  62
Foil-Baked Salmon, 262
Food processors:
  chipper disc, 134
  citrus press, 135
  dough hook, 132
    kit, 135
  juice extractor, 135
  plastic blade, 132
  shredding/grating disc, 133,
    142
  slicing disc, 132-133, 141
  steel blade, 131-132, 141
  whisk, 134
Freezer star ratings, 276
Freezing food, 216, 275 *et seq.*
Fresh Herb Dip, 121
Frozen fish, 216
  fruit, 63
  vegetables, 33, 87, 90, 176,
    225
Fruit, bottling, 235-237
  cakes, microwaving, 66
  , chopping with a blender,
    117
  , dried, 149, 232
  juice, blending, 120
  , microwaving, 63

, poached, 190
, pressure cooking, 229-232
, puréeing, 117, 229-230
, steaming, 97

G
Gammon, Glazed, 268
Garlic butter, 148
, freezing, 216
, processing, 143
, steaming, 92, 93
Gingerbread, 160
Glazed Gammon, 270
Globe artichokes, pressure
    cooking, 225
, steaming, 91
Golden Lemon Pudding, 201
Gooseberries, bottling, 237
, pressure cooking, 231
, processing, 144
Green beans, steaming, 91
Greengages, bottling, 237
, pressure cooking, 231
Grouse, pressure cooking, 221

H
Haddock, pressure cooking, 223
, Spicy, 261
, steaming, 95
Hake, pressure cooking, 223
Halibut, pressure cooking, 223
Ham, Cherry Tomato and
    Thyme Tart, 123
, pressure cooking, 220
Hare, pressure cooking, 221
Haricot beans, microwaving, 62
, pressure cooking, 227
Herb butter, 148
Dip, Fresh, 121
Herbs, chopping with a blender,
    118
Herrings, pressure cooking, 223

I
Ice, crushing, 120

J
Jam making, 234-235
Jerusalem artichokes, blanching,
    228
, pressure cooking, 225
, steaming, 91

K
Kidney beans, defrosting, 56
, microwaving, 58, 62

L
Lamb, defrosting, 56
Hotpot, 265
Korma, 73
, microwaving, 58
, Middle Eastern, 194
, pressure cooking, 220
, slow cooking, 186
, Spicy Casserole of, 157
, steaming, 96
with Leeks, Honey and
    Lemon, 106
Lasagne, reheating, 36, 37
, slow cooking, 177
Leeks, pressure cooking, 226
, processing, 143
, slow cooking, 188
, steaming, 93
Lemon curd, slow cooking, 191
Pudding, Golden, 201
Lentils, microwaving, 62
, pressure cooking, 227
Ling, pressure cooking, 223
Liver, defrosting, 56
, microwaving, 58
Pâté, Chicken, 154
Lobster, pressure cooking, 223
, steaming, 95
Loganberries, bottling, 237
, pressure cooking, 231

M
Mackerel, pressure cooking, 223
Mange tout, steaming, 93
Mango Lassi, 129

Marrow, pressure cooking, 226
, Stuffed, 269
Mayonnaise, 152
Meat, chopping with a blender, 117
, defrosting, 55-56, 87, 96
, microwaving, 56-58
pies, reheating, 37
, pressure cooking, 206, 219-221
, processing, 140-141
, slow cooking, 174, 185-186
, steaming, 88
Melting Moments, 274
Microwave cooking:
adapting your own recipes, 40 et seq.
advantages, 11-12
auto cook/heat, 21
auto-defrost, 21, 32-33
auto-minute button, 21
auto-repeat, 22
BEAB label, 16
browning agents, 44
browning dishes, 30, 43-44
cleaning, 38
cling film, 27, 48
combination oven, 22-23, 38
containers, 25 et seq.
controls, 20
defrosting, 32 et seq.
delay-start, 22
foil, 26
grill, 22
hold-warm, 21
labels, 23-24
leakage, 39
metal containers, 26
microwave bags, 27, 44
microwave rack, 30
microwave thermometer, 30, 34-35
minute timer, 21
plate ring, 30
power levels, 21, 47
quick start, 21
reheating, 36-37

replacement parts, 38
roasting bags, 27, 44
rotisserie units, 23
servicing, 39
shelf, 21, 41
turntable, 17, 20
wave stirrers, 20
Middle Eastern Lamb, 194
Milk puddings, microwaving, 64-65
, reheating, 37
Shakes, 128
Mocha Milk Shake, 128
Pots, 126
Monkfish, pressure cooking, 223
, steaming, 95
Moussaka, reheating, 37
Mousse, Strawberry Cream, 159
, White Chocolate, 76
Mullet, pressure cooking, 223
, steaming, 95
Mung beans, microwaving, 62
Mushroom Casserole, Chicken and, 195
, Pie, Potato and, 156
Sauce, 68
Mushrooms, processing, 143
, steaming, 93
Mussels, steaming, 95
Mustard Sauce, 68

N
Nectarines, steaming, 97
Nuts, chopping with a blender, 118

O
Onion Sauce, 68
Onions, pressure cooking, 226
, processing, 143
, slow cooking, 188
, steaming, 93
Oysters, steaming, 95

P
Pak choi, steaming, 93
Parsley Sauce, 68

Parsnips, blanching, 229
, pressure cooking, 226
, processing, 143
, slow cooking, 188
, steaming, 93
Partridge, pressure cooking, 221
Pasta, microwaving, 61-62
, slow cooking, 174, 177
, Tuna and Tomato, 67
Pastry, processing, 144-146
Pâté, Chicken Liver, 154
Pâtés, processing, 139
, slow cooking, 174, 191
Peach Cooler, 129
Peaches, bottling, 237
, pressure cooking, 232
, steaming, 97
with Almonds, Filled, 250
Pears, bottling, 235, 237
in Red Wine, 249
, pressure cooking, 231, 232
, slow cooking, 191
, steaming, 97
Peas, blanching, 229
, microwaving, 62
, pressure cooking, 226, 227
, steaming, 93
Pecan and Maple Syrup
Pudding, 107
Peppers, pressure cooking, 226
, processing, 143
, steaming, 93
Pheasant, slow cooking, 186
Pigeon, pressure cooking, 221
Pilchard and Tomato Loaf, 263
Pineapple, bottling, 237
Plaice, pressure cooking, 223
Rolls with Lemon and Spring
Onions, 102
, steaming, 95
Plum Clafoutis, 127
Plums, bottling, 237
, microwaving, 63
, pressure cooking, 231
, steaming, 97
Poaching fish, 187, 221-222
fruit, 190

Pork, defrosting, 56
in Cider, 267
in Foil – Greek Style, 105
in Sweet and Sour Sauce, 74
, microwaving, 58
, pressure cooking, 220
, slow cooking, 186
, steaming, 96
Potato and Mushroom Pie, 156
Potatoes, blanching, 229
, pressure cooking, 226
, processing, 143-144, 149
, reheating, 37
, slicing, 149
, slow cooking, 188, 189
, steaming, 93
Poultry, defrosting, 55-56, 87,
96, 216
, pressure cooking, 219, 220
, processing, 141
, reheating, 37, 44
, roasting in a fan oven, 259
, slow cooking, 174
, stuffing, 259
Prawn Sauce, 68
Sesame Sticks, 125
Prawns, defrosting, 52
, microwaving, 54
, pressure cooking, 223
, steaming, 96
Pressure cookers:
accessories, 209
audible pressure indicator,
212-213
choosing, 207
fixed pressure valve, 213-214
gasket, 215
reducing the pressure, 214
visual pressure indicator, 212,
213
Prunes, pressure cooking, 232
Pulses, microwaving, 61-62

Q
Queen of Puddings, 270

R

Rabbit, pressure cooking, 221
Radishes, processing, 144
Raspberries, bottling, 236, 237
, microwaving, 63
, pressure cooking, 232
, processing, 144
Red snapper, steaming, 95
Reheating food, 36-37
Rhubarb, bottling, 237
, microwaving, 63
, steaming, 97
Rice, microwaving, 61
, pressure cooking, 224
puddings, microwaving, 65
, Savoury, 199
, slow cooking, 174, 177
, steaming, 94
Roasting times, 186
Runner beans, 91

S

Salad dressings, blending, 119
Salmon, Foil-Baked, 262
Fries, 124
, steaming, 95
Sauce, blending, 115, 120
, White, 68, 120, 151
Sauces, defrosting, 55
, microwaving, 54-55
, processing, 140
, reheating, 37, 55
Sausage, Onion and Tomato
Casserole, 264
Sausages, steaming, 96
Savoury Rice, 199
Scallops, defrosting, 52
, microwaving, 54
, steaming, 96
Seafood Parcels, 103
Seakale, steaming, 93
Seeds, blending, 118
Shellfish, microwaving, 53
Shepherd's pie, reheating, 37
Shrimps, defrosting, 52
, pressure cooking, 223
Skate, pressure cooking, 223

Slow cooking:
browning method, 172-173
cooking liquid, 177
lid, 166
lifting strap, 180, 181
milk, 177
one-step method, 173
pot, 166-167
, fixed, 168
, removable, 168
settings, 168-169
stirring food, 174
Sole, pressure cooking, 223
, steaming, 95
Soup, blending, 115, 119
, Broccoli, 192
, Cock-a-Leekie, 243
, Cream of Cauliflower, 153
, Mixed Vegetable, 242
, pressure cooking, 217-218
, processing, 138-139
, slow cooking, 183-185
, Tomato, 69
with Soured Cream and Dill,
Beetroot, 122
Soups, microwaving, 50-51
, reheating, 37
Spicy Casserole of Lamb, 157
Haddock, 261
Spinach, blanching, 229
, pressure cooking, 226
, steaming, 93
Split peas, microwaving, 62
Sponge cakes, microwaving, 66
pudding, reheating, 36
, microwaving, 64
Squash Parcels with Brown
Sugar and Cinnamon, 100
, steaming, 94
Steamed puddings, 88, 173, 190,
232-234
Steaming:
bamboo steamer, 83
baskets, 82
electric steamers, 84-86
multi cookers, 84, 85
stand, 81

tiered steamers, 83-84
universal steamer, 82
Stock, 240
Strawberries, bottling, 236, 237
Strawberry and Vanilla Milk
    Shake, 128
    Cream Mousse, 159
Stuffed Marrow, 269
    Tomatoes, 198
Suet pudding, microwaving 63,
    64
Swedes, blanching, 229
    , pressure cooking, 226
    , processing, 144
    , slow cooking, 188
    , steaming, 94
Sweet and Sour Chicken, 158
    Sauce, Pork in, 74
Sweetcorn, blanching, 229
    , pressure cooking, 226
Swordfish, steaming, 95

T
Tart, Ham, Cherry Tomato and
    Thyme, 123
Tea-breads, slow cooking, 191
Thawing – see defrosting
Tipsy Apricots, 200
Tomato Soup, Fresh, 69
Tomatoes, processing, 144
    , Stuffed, 198
Trout and Almonds, 196
    , pressure cooking, 223
    , slow cooking, 187
    , steaming, 95

Tuna and Tomato Pasta, 67
    , steaming, 95
Turbot, pressure cooking, 223
Turkey, defrosting, 56
    Loaf, 266
    , microwaving, 58
Turnips, blanching, 229
    , food processing, 226
    , processing, 144
    , slow cooking, 188

V
Vanilla sugar, 120
Veal, pressure cooking, 220
    , slow cooking, 186
Vegetable Soup, Mixed, 242
Vegetables, blanching, 228
    , casseroling, 189
    , chopping with a blender,
        117
    , frozen, 33, 87, 90, 225
    in Cream Sauce, 75
    , microwaving, 59-61
    , pressure cooking, 224-229
    , processing, 141
    , puréeing with a blender, 117
    , reheating, 36
    , slow cooking, 176, 188-189
    , steaming, 88
Vegetarian Curry, 197
    Supper Loaf, 155
Venison, pressure cooking, 221

W
White Chocolate Mousse, 76
    Sauce, 68, 151
Whiting, pressure cooking, 223